T0327677

Trade
Stocks
and
Commodities
with the
Insiders

Founded in 1807, John Wiley & Sons is the oldest independent publishing company in the United States. With offices in North America, Europe, Australia, and Asia, Wiley is globally committed to developing and marketing print and electronic products and services for our customers' professional and personal knowledge and understanding.

The Wiley Trading series features books by traders who have survived the market's ever changing temperament and have prospered—some by reinventing systems, others by getting back to basics. Whether a novice trader, professional, or somewhere in-between, these books will provide the advice and strategies needed to prosper today and well into the future.

For a list of available titles, visit our web site at www.WileyFinance.com.

Trade Stocks and Commodities with the Insiders

Secrets of the COT Report

LARRY WILLIAMS

WILEY

John Wiley & Sons, Inc.

Published by John Wiley & Sons, Inc., Hoboken, New Jersey.
Published simultaneously in Canada.

For general information on our other products and services or for technical support, please
contact our Customer Care Department within the United States at (800) 762-2974, outside
the United States at (317) 572-3993 or fax (317) 572-4002.

Wiley also publishes its books in a variety of electronic formats. Some content that appears
in print may not be available in electronic books. For more information about Wiley
products, visit our web site at www.wiley.com.

Library of Congress Cataloging-in-Publication Data:
Williams, Larry R.
    Trade stocks & commodities with the insiders : secrets of the COT report
  / Larry Williams.
        p.   cm. — (Wiley trading series)
    Includes index.
    ISBN-13: 978-0-471-74125-1 (cloth)
    ISBN-10: 0-471-74125-6 (cloth)
  1. Stocks.   2. Commodity futures.   3. Speculation.   I. Title: Trade
stocks and commodities with the insiders.   II. Title.   III. Series.
    HG6041.W497   2005
    332.64—dc22

                                                              2005007674

Printed in the United States of America.

10   9   8   7   6   5   4   3   2   1

Contents

Introduction

Warning: Futures trading, stock trading, currency trading, options trading, etc., involve high risk and you can lose a lot of money.

What a way to start an introduction to a book! Those scary words are just one of the current disclaimers the Federal Trade Commission (FTC) has proposed be prominently displayed by anyone offering an investment course to the public. Who can argue with that statement? Certainly not I.

However, two points are missing here. The first is obvious: if someone is losing money in the market, by the very definition, someone else is making money. Every dollar lost is a dollar won by someone else, hopefully you or me. There is another side of the coin the FTC does not want you to see: the potential for gargantuan profits. Where else have millions been made, in less time, with less work and less dollars up front?

What your mom or dad told you is correct. Without risk there is not much to be gained; risk and reward go hand in hand with each other. If there were no risk involved we could not have the potential for gain. To get rewards, we need risks. Duh!

When the markets first intrigued you, did you think it was possible to lose money? I sure thought it was, so the gummint men are just restating what we already know. Or are they just suppressive people at heart?

The second point I have is even more egregious. How come I have to state the obvious in an ad I choose to run, while in today's *Investor's Business Daily* (*IBD*) the exchanges-backed "Options University" is not required to scare away would-be options players? Or why doesn't a subscription to the *Wall Street Journal, Forbes, BusinessWeek,* or *IBD* come with the same warning? Why aren't brokerage firms required to use these same words?

The only reason I know of is that this is a rigged business.

The exchanges, the brokerage firms, and the large funds have set the table for themselves, created rules for themselves that are different from the rules for the smaller players in the game. There is one set of rules for what they can do and another for the average trader or adviser.

Frankly, I have no problem with that. It's their game, and they have the marbles. But we need to know of those differences to not get sucked into their game. To win at this game you need to not only know the rules but not be trapped into the fallacies. To that end let me expose a few of them.

FIRST FALLACY—"THESE GUYS KNOW SOMETHING"

In 2000 the *Wall Street Journal* survey of economists revealed that 96 percent of them were bullish.

In 2001 the same surveys of economists showed an amazing 99 percent were bullish on the economy.

In 2002, the same survey was conducted again, and by now 100 percent of the economists surveyed were bullish.

The *Wall Street Journal* has been doing this survey thing since 1982, and the track record shows the experts have been correct in predicting the future less than 22 percent of the time. This is a worse probability than random guessing!

Yet they continue doing the survey and not telling you how horrible these guys' predictions have been.

The *London Financial Times* (*LFT*) did a study in 1995 that stated, "Consensus economic forecasts failed to predict any of the most important developments in the economy over the last seven years."

SECOND FALLACY—"IF THEY KNEW SOMETHING, THEY'D TELL YOU"

Forty-three years ago, when I began following stocks, I was sure a brokerage firm could and would help me a lot. After all, wasn't that what they were in business for? Finally I got it; they are in business to make money (generate commissions) and despite what they say or do, brokers that generate huge commissions get huge rewards. The incentive is all about commissions, not customers.

Doubt that? Then explain away that Citicorp, Merrill Lynch, and a few of the other big boys were fined $1.4 billion for issuing biased ratings on stocks to lure investors.

Hmm . . . why didn't the FTC have them place all those warning labels on their ads and their golf and tennis tournament promotions?

MY WAKE-UP CALL

Many years ago it was also Merrill Lynch that was fined a few hundred million for telling customers to buy when they were selling. If you and I do that, we end up in jail; they do it and they get to sponsor a conference on the new economy and give more money to politicians.

What I learned is that we are very much in this game on our own. It's really the little guys and gals, like you and me, against the establishment. At every turn it is set up for them, not us. Me? I kinda like that—us against them—but until you come to that realization you will play the game like they are on your side. The evidence, the facts, and the fines indicate otherwise.

There . . . that's what the FTC should be telling everyone!

There is one thing you have been told, though, that is true; there are people who know more about the markets than you. Lots more. You've searched high and low for these people, and thought brokers or the media would dredge up their advice. Wake up, Charley, that's not the way the game works.

THE SUPERPOWERS

What you are about to learn is that there are true superpowers of the marketplace, so critical to market structure they are required, by federal law, to report their massive buying and selling once every week.

If they don't report they will be hit with massive fines and/or go to jail. Imagine how influential these guys are! Imagine what might happen if one whispered in your ear what he was buying. Is that information you could use?

I suspect only one investor or trader out of 10,000 is aware of this vital information, posted, for free, on the Internet every week. Most investors are looking at charts instead of the buying and selling of the people who move the charts.

Let me be clear here. I am not talking about employees in a company or officers and directors. While it's true they might time some of their buys and sells rather well (Bill Gates and Paul Allen sure did), an employee or officer may sell to take profits, not because he foresees lower prices. Indeed, what he foresees is braces or college tuition for the kids, or a divorce.

Nor will I bore you with what the mutual funds are buying, for one simple reason: 85 percent of mutual funds don't do as well for you as if you had just bought the laggard Dow Jones Industrial Average stocks. Amazing but true, only 15 percent of all funds outperform the simple strategy of buying and holding the Dow Industrials! What makes this even more remarkable is that it is not always the same 15 percent of funds that outperform the market. Funds come into and out of this list of success faster than rap songs hit and fall off the charts.

No, I'm going to be talking about what the largest, most powerful corporations are doing with their money, money they have to invest in their business every week of the year, year in and year out to maximize their profits.

I have been following this smart money crowd since 1970. More than 30 years of tracking these astute financial powers have taught me things I can teach you. In these years I have learned that while this camp of investors/traders is not always right, they consistently make the best bets in the game.

It was my lucky day in 1969 when a fellow named Bill Meehan was introduced to me by a couple of traders in the San Jose, California, area. Those two, Chet Conrad and Keith Campbell, went on to amazing success. The last I heard of Keith he was managing well over $1 billion, and Chet has parlayed his market winnings into an even more sure bet: he bought a casino in Reno. I have not seen Chet or the Campbells since the early 1970s. We have all gone our own way to do our own thing. All three of us owe a debt of gratitude to Bill for teaching us what he knew.

Bill, a former member of the Chicago Board of Trade, was kind enough, for a fee, to teach me how he followed these superpowers. Bill looked at this group with several sets of data, but the most powerful was something called the "Commitment of Traders" (COT) report. Back then, this report was released one month after the superpowers had bought or sold, so it was a bit delayed. Still, though, it had great merit. Today the report is released every week with a delay of just a few days.

When most people think of investing, they think of stocks and bonds. That's traditional thinking. What they are not aware of is that each day about five times more dollars change hands in the commodity markets. Traditional real estate or stock investors are missing the boat. They are quite literally on a small boat in a small pond compared to the physical commodity markets.

Did someone say a dirty word? "Aren't commodities full of risk?" you ask. To which I candidly admit yes, for sure, but no more risk than stocks, as you will soon see. Commodities, in the past, were to be joked about. They were an investment arena for only the bravest or most foolish, depending on your view. That has changed greatly since I first traded pork bellies in 1968. As the world has changed so have the markets. A new breed of commodities appeared consisting of financial instruments, such as bonds, Treasury bills, currencies, and stock market indexes like the Dow Jones Industrials and the S&P 500. We were no longer trading eggs and orange juice (the breakfast spread) or cattle and wheat (the dinner spread).

Overnight banks, governments, and worldwide corporations began using the commodity markets to protect their business interests. If General Motors was selling cars to Japan, they needed to make certain the value of their payment in the future in yen did not collapse between now and when they were to be paid. The superpowers entered the commodity markets, and the trading pits in Chicago have never been the same since. Long gone are the days of one or two large traders "running" a market. No one individual has the money and backing of any one of the commercials.

The commercials, the superpowers, have research staffs, people in the field learning all they can about a physical commodity such as wheat, gold, corn, and the like as well as the abstract commodities (the manmade ones) like the British pound, the yen, Treasury bonds, the S&P 500 stock index, or other market indexes from around the world.

Whenever the commercials trade they leave tracks—the record of their buying and selling. Those are tracks we can easily follow. They are the tracks of what real informed players in the game are doing with their own real money!

This is the great advantage a commodity speculator has; he or she can rely on inside information legally, something a stock guy or gal can never do.

I say that because the weekly COT report reveals to us all the buying and selling these powerhouse players have been doing. It then becomes our job to understand what their actions mean and align ourselves with them. That's what this book is about . . . getting in step, investing and trading side by side with the largest commercial interests in the world.

HISTORICAL PERSPECTIVE ON COMMODITY AND FUTURES TRADING

What we know as the commodity markets of today came from some humble beginnings. Trading in futures originated in Japan during the eighteenth century and was primarily used for the trading of rice and silk. It wasn't until the 1850s that the United States started using futures markets to buy and sell commodities such as cotton, corn, and wheat.

A futures contract is a type of derivative instrument, or financial contract, in which two parties agree to transact a set of financial instruments or physical commodities for future delivery at a particular price. If you buy a futures contract, you are basically agreeing to buy something, for a set price, that a seller has not yet produced. But participating in the futures market does not necessarily mean that you will be responsible for receiving or delivering large inventories of physical commodities—remember, buyers and sellers in the futures market primarily enter into futures contracts to hedge risk or speculate rather than exchange physical goods (which is the primary activity of the cash/spot market). That is why futures are used as financial instruments not only by producers and consumers but also by speculators.

Before the North American futures market originated some 150 years ago, farmers would grow their crops and then bring them to market in the hope of selling their inventory. But without any indication of demand, supply often exceeded what was needed, and crops that were not bought were left to rot in the streets! Conversely, when a given commodity—for instance, wheat—was out of season, the goods made from it became very expensive because the crop was no longer available. Bread was cheap in the fall and dear in the springtime.

In the mid-nineteenth century, central grain markets were established and a central marketplace was created for farmers so they might bring their commodities and sell them either for immediate delivery (spot trading) or for forward delivery. The latter contracts—forward contracts, contracts dealing with the future—were the forerunners to today's futures contracts. This innovative concept saved many a farmer the loss of crops and profits and helped stabilize supply and prices in the off-season.

While futures are not for the risk-averse, they are useful for a wide range of people trying to break out of the humdrum 9 to 5 job syndrome, people like me who believe we should remain independent of any source of income that will deprive us of our personal liberties.

ACKNOWLEDGMENTS

There have been many people who have kept me in step with life and the markets, like Bill Meehan, who first lectured me on the commercials in 1969. I'd like to thank my long-term buddies and dear friends—Tom De-Mark, Harvey Levine, Richard Joseph, and the best partner I have ever had, Louise Stapleton, without whose love and attention to details this book would never have seen the light of day. A special thanks to Chris LeDoux, whom I never met but whose music has been inspirational to my trading and living. Also a note of appreciation to Brian Schaad for all the help with my newsletter, my personal assistant Jennifer Wells, Carla for always caring when she no longer has to, and above all my five children, who each in their own way have shown me how to walk . . . and dance to the joys of more than stocks and shares.

L. W.

St. Croix, U.S. Virgin Islands
2005

CHAPTER 1

Meet Your New Investment Partner and Adviser

Commercials are for more than television.

The sole purpose of this book is to get you in investment alignment with the billion-dollar successful traders and pools that move in and out of the marketplace. They will become more than your mentor; they will become your investment partner, whispering in their own way to you each week where they have been placing their money. I will be teaching you who these people are, and several ways to follow them to add to your understanding of how markets work.

While most market followers look at charts, you will be looking at the actual condition that affects price change: large buying and selling, true supply/demand pressure that we will be able to see each week as the billion-dollar successful traders and pools enter the marketplace.

Since these guys are our partners, let's meet them. Let's find out all we can about this group of traders so respected—and feared—they must register with the U.S. government and reveal all their market actions. A karate fighter having to register his powerful fists at the local police station is a good analogy.

The government in this case means the Commodity Futures Trading Commission (CFTC). Here's a little more about who they are and what they are supposed to do. The mission of the CFTC is to protect market users and the public from fraud, manipulation, and abusive practices related to the sale of commodity and financial futures and options, and to foster open, competitive, and financially sound futures and option markets.

1

Futures contracts for agricultural commodities have been traded in the United States for more than 150 years and have been under federal regulation since the 1920s. In recent years, trading in futures contracts has expanded rapidly beyond traditional physical and agricultural commodities into a vast array of financial instruments, including foreign currencies, U.S. and foreign government securities, and U.S. and foreign stock indexes.

EVOLVING MISSION AND RESPONSIBILITIES

Congress created the CFTC in 1974 as an independent agency with the mandate to regulate commodity futures and option markets in the United States. The agency's mandate has been renewed and expanded several times since then, most recently by the Commodity Futures Modernization Act of 2000 (CFMA). Today, the CFTC ensures the economic utility of the futures markets by encouraging their competitiveness and efficiency; ensuring their integrity; protecting market participants against manipulation, abusive trading practices, and fraud; and ensuring the financial integrity of the clearing process. Through effective oversight, the CFTC enables the futures markets to serve the important function of providing a means for price discovery and offsetting price risk.

HOW THE CFTC IS ORGANIZED

The CFTC consists of five commissioners appointed by the U.S. President to serve staggered five-year terms. The President, with the consent of the Senate, designates one of the commissioners to serve as chairman. No more than three commissioners at any one time may be from the same political party.

The chairman's staff has direct responsibility for providing information about the Commission to the public and interacting with other governmental agencies and the Congress, and for the preparation and dissemination of Commission documents. The chairman's staff also ensures that the CFTC is responsive to requests filed under the Freedom of Information Act. The chairman's staff includes the Office of the Inspector General, which conducts audits of CFTC programs and operations, and the Office of International Affairs, which is the focal point for the CFTC's global regulatory coordination efforts.

The Chairman's staff is also responsible for liaison with the public, the Congress, and the media. The Office of External Affairs (OEA) is the CFTC's liaison with the domestic and foreign news media, producer and market user groups, educational and academic groups and institutions, and the general public. The OEA provides timely and relevant information about the Commission's regulatory mandate, the economic role of the futures markets, new market instruments, market regulation, enforcement actions, and customer protection initiatives, actions, and issues. The OEA also provides assistance to members of the media and the general public accessing the CFTC's Internet web site (www.cftc.gov).

The CFTC monitors markets and market participants closely by maintaining, in addition to its headquarters office in Washington, offices in cities that have futures exchanges—New York, Chicago, Kansas City, and Minneapolis.

By law, traders must register and report their activities, and by law, the CFTC issues reports where you will learn to read what your soon-to-be partners as hedgers are doing. We will further identify them as taking positions in the market for commercial purposes as opposed to those who use the markets for speculation. These are truly the large players in the market. In fact, while you or I or a group of traders known as "large traders" can own only so much of a commodity, the hedgers or commercials (our partners in all this) have no limit to how much of a commodity they can buy or sell.

That means when the commercials see an opportunity in the markets they can step up to the plate and buy millions of pounds, bushels, or contracts of a commodity. They are the best-capitalized players in the game. They have the deepest pockets and one core reason to be in the markets: they actually use or produce the product. It is their professional business to buy and sell; they know the markets better than the outsiders, you and I. Here's an analogy. I'm not too keen on cars and never learned much about mechanical things. So if I'm going to buy a new car I can read up on cars, then talk to a salesperson, and perhaps even take a test-drive (sorry, no test-drives in the marketplace) to arrive at a somewhat informed decision.

Or, if I happen to personally know Roy Stanley, the owner of the local Chevy dealership, I can cut to the quick and ask him what's best for me. He's in the business of knowing cars, the business of buying and selling them. He's an insider in his world, so I treasure his advice.

The commercials seemingly have unlimited resources. Bill Meehan (see Introduction) told me they usually account for 60 percent of the volume in a market, so it pays to respect their judgment, to covet their wisdom, and to pay attention to what they do. To them the markets are a business, not a speculation.

The very bottom line for the commercials is that they attempt to minimize their losses as opposed to us speculators, who attempt to make profits. Let me explain. A commercial has an inventory of the product or needs the product. His or her trading will be around the product—the need to buy it or sell it. If a commercial in, say sugar, knows his company will need a million pounds of sugar in the next month and he believes sugar prices are going higher, he is literally forced to step in and buy now, today. By the same token if he thinks sugar is due for a decline—lower prices—he will still buy some sugar because he needs it to make cotton candy or whatever. But he will not be as aggressive in his buying, and we can pick up on that in the weekly CFTC report.

Here's the unusual thing that has perplexed many followers of the commercials. In an extended decline they will buy all the way down. Hence, it looks like they are dumb as they bought at high prices. "Dumb as foxes," I say. The cheaper our friend can buy sugar, the more profit he has in his cotton candy as his base cost of the product is reduced by the lower sugar cost.

My point is the commercials are not like you and me. They buy to use the product or to protect against a sudden change in prices, to lock in a profit as a producer of the item. You and I, dear reader, have a different function. Our task is to buy low and sell high, to make money from market swings while our commercial mentors are using the markets to make money in their businesses.

We can sure as heck use these guys in our game plan, as when they get unusually bullish or bearish the markets are most likely to have major moves, often with the potential for making millions of dollars. I know—I have done just that in sync with the commercials, just as Bill Meehan showed us.

You and I have one large advantage over the commercials. They must transact in the marketplace every day. It is a permanent business for them. Day in, day out, they have to be doing their best to protect their positions. That's not true of us! We can come in and out of the markets at our fancy. We have the luxury of waiting, with great patience, for the perfect time, a time when the commercials have become uniformly biased and have become massive buyers or sellers in anticipation of a major market move.

Let me also add this: we live in an imperfect world. At times the commercials may be wrong or at least on a short-term basis appear to be on the wrong side of a market. I'm sure they don't want to be wrong. The future, however, is fragile and oh so hard to forecast correctly. If they were always right we'd all become instant millionaires, and what fun would that be?

Because they can be wrong, at least for a while, we need tools and tactics to protect our hard-earned speculative dollars from being taken from us. In later chapters I get into some of the techniques I use to make certain that my entry and exit points, as well as my money management, are effectively used to protect against the risk of ruin.

Nothing is for sure in the world of speculation; the commercials sometimes buy a little early, and with their deeper pockets it does not matter to them. But most of us with shallower pockets, or none at all, will need more precise entry levels and absolute control of our losses.

There are three primary classes of trading action we can see each week: the hedgers or commercials, large traders (large speculators), and small traders (small speculators). These groups all look at the same market yet act differently, as the market serves different missions for each of them.

Some traders are speculators and some are hedgers. Speculators expect the price to go up when they buy a contract and expect the price to go down when they sell a contract. The idea for speculators is to buy low, sell high, and make a profit on the difference. Large hedgers that are users want to buy at low prices, whereas large hedgers that are producers want to sell at high prices. The idea for hedgers is to guarantee some price they will get or give for the commodity, currency, or financial security they're trading.

Consider for a moment that you are a wheat farmer. You estimate you will produce about 50,000 bushels of wheat and that it will cost you close to $3.25 a bushel to grow the wheat and get it to a grain terminal to sell. One fine day you open up your local paper and see that wheat, for delivery in December, is selling for $4.10 a bushel. It's May and your crop is in the ground. The current price of wheat means you can make 85 cents per bushel if you sell in the market now against what you know you can deliver by December. Your profit would be $42,500 ($.85 times the 50,000 bushels), but there are problems.

First, what if your crop fails? Maybe there will be a drought, "hoppers" will eat it alive, or you will get hailed on just before harvest. Then you won't be able to deliver all 50,000 bushels and might have a problem if wheat is selling for more than $4.10 a bushel when it is time to deliver the contract. If you can't deliver the wheat, you will have to fork over the difference between what you sold it for and the current price.

By the same token, if wheat goes down in price and by the time delivery rolls around it is selling for less than $4.10 a bushel, you have made yourself a profit (the current price minus what you sold it for). Of course, the fact you don't have wheat to deliver usually means a lot of other ranches don't have wheat to deliver. A shortage of a crop such as that usually means higher prices.

Also, what if wheat prices rally to $8.10 a bushel and you could have sold at that price, making $4.85 a bushel for a net gain of $242,500? Ahh . . . you city slickers can see there is more to farming than running a tractor. For all these reasons, and a few more, a producer, be it wheat or gold, beans or bacon, will want to use the futures markets, but with care.

And now you can appreciate that if wheat starts to rally you will sell some of your crop at different price levels. At $4.10 a bushel you may sell one-tenth of your crop, at $5.00 a bushel you may sell another one-third, and by then you may know how abundant your harvest will be so you may decide to sell more at $6.00 and the rest of it at $7.00 a bushel.

You're happy as a hog in slop. You sold your entire crop at prices higher than your cost. You do not care if wheat goes to $20 a bushel, though you will curse yourself for selling too soon. The weekly CFTC report will reflect your selling. If lots of farmers sold wheat at say $5 a bushel and it rallies to $10 it will look like dumb selling. But was it? The farmers were happy to sell at that price. They took a profit.

One of the important features of futures markets is the interaction between speculators and hedgers. Since speculators have different opinions about how prices will move, speculators may buy and sell contracts to each other. Also, hedgers who are producers want to guarantee the price they will get for what they're trading, and hedgers who are processors want to guarantee the price they will have to pay.

Since producers and processors both want to guarantee what return they will get or price they will pay or be paid, hedgers may buy and sell contracts between each other. However, contracts between traders are more often between speculators and hedgers.

When price goes up, speculators want to buy more contracts and producers want to sell more of what they're trading. This is an important law of the jungle we live in.

When price goes down, speculators want to sell more contracts and processors want to buy more of what they're trading. Think of the mind-set of the speculator who is trying to make money from the current downtrend; his or her bet is it will continue, so he or she sells short in the hope that prices will go down more and profits will accrue.

Meanwhile, the mind-set of the commercial hedger is quite different. The commercial is not trying (almost always) to make money from what the market is doing, but rather from the current price of the market or commodity. If the commercials see a price that is lower than they've been paying, they're tempted to buy, as now the cost of the product they make with the commodity is lower; hence the markup is better than it was when the cost of production was higher when the commodity cost more.

Does the commercial care if the trend continues and prices go still lower? No, not really; if prices go lower they have not lost money, as they buy to take delivery (in one form or another). The fact prices decline has no bearing on the excess profits they will make from their purchase, as their profits come from the markup on the product they make from the commodity.

If prices go lower they will want to buy more. What all commercial producers would like to see would be a product cost of zero, and then all they would have to worry about is the cost of production—the cost of turning corn into cornflakes, wheat into bread.

Every futures market has a different mix of speculators and hedgers. Some markets, like financial markets, are dominated by hedgers buying and selling with one another; and others, like many commodities, are dominated by speculators buying and selling with other speculators.

However, most markets have speculators and hedgers on opposite sides of most contracts. This is an important point and one we will deal with at length when it comes to market timing and selection of what market to position ourselves in.

Hedgers in futures markets are called commercial traders, while speculators are called noncommercial traders. All futures contracts are registered with the CFTC, the government regulatory authority for the industry. The cost for registering contracts is higher for speculators than for hedgers. Consequently, those traders who are producing or processing large amounts of whatever they are trading register as commercial traders, while all other traders are either large noncommercial traders with many contracts traded at a time or other traders with only a few contracts traded at a time.

The CFTC assembles a list of the contracts registered every day by each trader category in about 75 markets and publishes them every week on the Internet at www.cftc.gov. This report is called "Commitments of Traders" (COT) and includes open interest for commercial buyers and sellers, large noncommercial buyers and sellers, and other buyers and sellers (little guys, the public). From these reports it is possible to see how many contracts are held by commercial buyers and sellers—the big guys, our buddies.

What's the world's largest trading market? Immense as it is, it's not the stock market, and it's not bonds or commodities.

No, the world's leading market is, believe it not, the currency exchange. In trading volume, daily currency exchange turnover now exceeds US$1.5 trillion—more than 50 times greater than the New York Stock Exchange, the world's largest securities market. I told you these guys are superpowers, and the math of the marketplace sure drives home that point.

Many people think currency trading is only for the wealthy. That's not true. What is true is that superpowers are the big players and there is no other market that offers the potential to create great wealth in a relatively short period of time such as the currency markets offer. With the right guidance and following the right crowd, you can trade these markets very effectively with a modest account of US$10,000 or US$20,000, sometimes less.

In should be noted that in January 2005 the CFTC made a nominal change in reporting requirements, telling us:

> *The Commodity Futures Trading Commission has amended its large trader reporting rules. The large trader reporting rules require futures commission merchants, clearing members, foreign brokers, and traders to report certain position and identifying information to the Commission when the positions of traders equal or exceed Commission set contract reporting levels. The final rules, among other things, raise contract reporting levels, and as a result, impact the reports provided by the Commission on the* Commitments of Traders *(COT).*
>
> *The Commission typically calibrates contract reporting levels so that the aggregate of all positions reported to the Commission represents approximately 70 to 90 percent of the total open interest in any given contract. The Commission periodically reviews information concerning trading volume, open interest, its surveillance experience with specific contracts, and the number and position sizes of individual traders relative to the reporting levels for each contract to determine if coverage of open interest is adequate for effective market surveillance. COT data provides a breakdown of each Tuesday's open interest for markets in which twenty or more traders hold positions that equal or exceed Commission set contract reporting levels. COT reports categorize positions as reportable or nonreportable, and provide additional information for reportable positions. The raised contract reporting levels alter the number of reportable positions and the information that is provided on such positions in COT reports. Persons that rely on COT reports should be aware of the impact of the raised contract reporting levels.*

WHO OUR BUDDIES ARE

Our buddies, the guys the United States government labels the commercials, are often household names. You will be keying off the buying and selling of corporations like Pillsbury, General Mills, Cargill, Iowa Beef, and Nabisco when it comes to understanding the natural resource commodities. In all aspects of commercial or financial life there are companies or organizations that have made it their business to know, so they can survive and prosper, the true economic status of one particular market: the one they are engaged in.

When it comes to the abstract or financial commodities, we will be queuing up with the likes of JP Morgan Chase, General Motors, and Microsoft along with all of the world's largest banks and brokerage firms. These people must hedge currency in interest rates, and do so on a daily basis—in positions large enough that they must be reported to the CFTC. Isn't that nice of them!

What is true today was just as true decades ago. The following comments from almost a quarter of a century ago by Bill Jiler, developer of the widely followed Commodity Research Bureau Index of commodity prices, need not have one word altered or removed; the powers then were the same as they are today. These comments are from his paper "The Forecasting Methodology," written in 1985.

Basically, we tried to determine the "forecasting" performance of the major identifiable groups of market participants—Large Hedgers, Large Speculators, and Small Traders. It was logical to assume that the larger and more sophisticated traders should have market insights that would enable them to predict futures price movements, if not infallibly, at least more accurately than the small traders who presumably included the "uninformed public." We also thought it was possible that the sizes of the various market positions, at different times, could well result in a type of self-fulfilling prophecy.

From the statistics in the "Commitments of Traders" report, we were able to approximate the net positions at the end of each month for Large Hedgers, Large Speculators, and Small Traders. We averaged their month-end statistics over a number of years to find out what their normal positions would be at any given time of the year. We then compared each group's actual position with their so-called normal position. Whenever their positions deviated materially from the norm, we took it as a measure of their bullish or bearish attitude on the market.

By studying subsequent price movements, we were able to establish "track records" for each of the groups. As anticipated, we found that Large Hedgers and Large Speculators had the best forecasting records, and the Small Traders the worst, by far. We were somewhat surprised to find that the Large Hedgers were consistently superior to the Large Speculators. However, the predictive results for the Large Speculators varied widely from market to market.

The differences between their current net open interest position and the seasonal norm supply us with a tangible percentage measure of the degree of bullishness or bearishness of each group towards a particular market to a certain extent. From these "net-net" figures, we obtain a configuration of market attitudes of the principal players. From our research and long experience we have drawn up some general guidelines:

The most bullish configuration would show Large Hedgers heavily net long more than normal, Large Speculators clearly net long, Small Traders heavily net short more than seasonal. The shades of bullishness are varied all the way to the most bearish configuration which would have these groups in opposite positions—large hedgers heavily net short, etc. There are two caution flags when analyzing deviations from normal. Be wary of positions that are more than 40% from their long-term average and disregard deviations of less than 5%.

We'd like to present some examples of how we utilized this open interest analysis in our "Technical Comments" section of the CRB Futures Chart Service. In late August of 1983, we turned bearish on sugar when it was over 10¢ a pound. Throughout 1983 and 1984, we advocated a bearish stand even though prices had dropped below 4¢ to 16-year lows. An important reason for our doggedness, in addition to the bearish chart, was our analysis of the "Commitments" report. For over two years, the Large Hedgers' average net short position was over 20% larger than their previous 6-year average. Small Traders, despite tremendous losses, averaged almost 20% higher net long positions throughout the entire debacle.

In August of 1983, Chicago wheat futures soared to new contract highs. The charts were very bullish, which we acknowledged in our "Comments" of August 12, 1983. However, we noted that the latest "Commitments of Traders" report sounded a negative note. Large Hedgers were 36% net short and Small Traders were 24% net long, both way over their 10-year averages at that time. Subsequently, the market topped out and prices trended lower for the next 6 months.

A study of the open interest configuration for corn and soybeans just prior to their spectacular bull move in the summer of 1983 will show how the analysis "did" and "didn't" work. It worked for corn, which showed Large Hedgers with net long positions well above normal and Small Traders net short. This bullish pattern was just the opposite of the soybean open interest. Here, Large Hedgers were heavily net short and Small Traders had a net long position of 20% versus a more normal 10% for June. Yet, both commodities enjoyed similar bull moves. An unforeseen drought that summer probably accounted for the strange results.

While we have shown only some relatively recent examples of this kind of open interest analysis, our experience with the technique goes back over two decades. The performance patterns are fairly consistent. Yet, we have to admit that there were exceptions that proved to be quite dramatic. Therefore, it is important also to utilize other available technical and fundamental tools to arrive at a high probability of success in forecasting prices. The nature of the events that shape price trends of futures contracts should keep even the most proficient of technical and fundamental analysts on their guard and flexible at all times. International developments, weather, and politically-motivated legislation are among the unpredictable forces that can change the direction of the markets in an instant. There is no master key that can unlock all the doors to successful price forecasting. Nevertheless, we believe that the proper interpretation of the "Commitments of Traders" reports is valuable and belongs on the analyst's key ring.

To best use the data from the commercials, recall the line from the song "Rawhide": "Don't try to understand them, just rope and tie and brand them." As you will see, it's pretty simple to follow the commercials. There are no labyrinths to explore or complex matrixes to crawl through; just know these guys play the game better than anyone else.

They're pretty good company to keep, these mega-powers of commerce and industry!

Next let's learn how to follow them. . . .

CHAPTER 2

Watching the Commercials

Throw away your channel changer.

Every week the Commodity Futures Trading Commission (CFTC) releases the buying and selling done the prior week by the three camps or crowds mentioned in Chapter 1. The official release is made at www.cftc.gov. There is a lot of information there that we will distill down into some specific trading tools.

But, for openers, here's the way the report looks and what the government has to say about it:

> *The first* Commitments of Traders *(COT) report was published for 13 agricultural commodities as of June 30, 1962. At the time, this report was proclaimed as "another step forward in the policy of providing the public with current and basic data on futures market operations." Those original reports were compiled on an end-of-month basis and were published on the 11th or 12th calendar day of the following month.*
>
> *Over the years, in a continuous effort to better inform the public about futures markets, the Commodity Futures Trading Commission has improved the COT in several ways. The COT report is published more often—switching to mid-month and month-end in 1990, to every 2 weeks in 1992, and to weekly in 2000. The COT report is released more quickly—moving the publication to the 6th business day after the "as of" date (1990) and then to the 3rd business day after the "as of" date (1992). The report includes more information— adding data on the numbers of traders in each category, a crop-year*

breakout, and concentration ratios (early 1970s) and data on option positions (1995). The report also is more widely available—moving from a subscription-based mailing list to fee-based electronic access (1993) to being freely available on the Commission's Internet website (1995).

The COT reports provide a breakdown of each Tuesday's open interest for markets in which 20 or more traders hold positions equal to or above the reporting levels established by the CFTC. The weekly reports for Futures-Only Commitments of Traders *and for* Futures-and-Options-Combined Commitments of Traders *are released every Friday at 3:30 p.m. Eastern time.*

Reports are available in both a short and long format. The short report shows open interest separately by reportable and nonreportable positions. For reportable positions, additional data are provided for commercial and non-commercial holdings, spreading, changes from the previous report, percents of open interest by category, and numbers of traders. The long report, in addition to the information in the short report, also groups the data by crop year, where appropriate, and shows the concentration of positions held by the largest four and eight traders.

Current and historical Commitments of Traders *data are available on the Internet at the Commission's website:* http://www.cftc.gov. *Also available at that site are historical COT data going back to 1986 for futures-only reports and to 1995 for option-and-futures-combined reports.*

Example

A page from the June 1, 2004, COT report (short format) showing data for the Chicago Board of Trade's wheat futures contract is depicted [in Table 2.1]. Explanatory notes follow the table.

What follows next in the report are definitions from the CFTC to help us better understand what all these numbers mean. There are more numbers than most of us care to deal with, and unless you know how to use these numbers they become an effort in futility and frustration. Later in this chapter I begin to show you how I use this information. I simplify it for you, yet I think it is important you wade through the explanations so you really do understand the construction of the numbers and how they come about.

Here are important definitions of the parts that make up the whole of these reports. The better you understand the terms, the better you will be able to understand the markets and how the commercials are the driving force of the markets . . . and our profits.

TABLE 2.1 Sample "Commitments of Traders" Report

WHEAT -- CHICAGO BOARD OF TRADE

FUTURES-ONLY POSITIONS AS OF 06/01/2004

NONCOMMERCIAL			COMMERCIAL		TOTAL		NONREPORTABLE POSITIONS	
LONG	SHORT	SPREADS	LONG	SHORT	LONG	SHORT	LONG	SHORT
(CONTRACTS OF 5,000 BUSHELS)		OPEN INTEREST: 122,975						
COMMITMENTS								
29,015	29,513	9,514	67,135	60,224	105,664	99,251	17,311	23,724
CHANGES FROM 05/25/2004	CHANGE IN OPEN INTEREST: -963							
-2,090	-3,837	-2,472	3,005	6,132	-1,557	-177	594	-786
PERCENT OF OPEN INTEREST FOR EACH CATEGORY OF TRADERS								
23.6	24.0	7.7	54.6	49.0	85.9	80.7	14.1	19.3
NUMBER OF TRADERS IN EACH CATEGORY	(TOTAL TRADERS: 234)							
66	81	54	46	61	150	169		

Source: Commodity Futures Trading Commission (www.cftc.gov).

Explanatory Notes

Open Interest—*Open interest is the total of all futures and/or option contracts entered into and not yet offset by a transaction, by delivery, by exercise, etc. The aggregate of all long open interest is equal to the aggregate of all short open interest. Open interest held or controlled by a trader is referred to as that trader's position. For the* COT Futures & Options Combined *report, option open interest and traders' option positions are computed on a futures-equivalent basis using delta factors supplied by the exchanges. Long-call and short-put open interest are converted to long futures-equivalent open interest. Likewise, short-call and long-put open interest are converted to short futures-equivalent open interest. For example, a trader holding a long put position of 500 contracts with a delta factor of 0.50 is considered to be holding a short futures-equivalent position of 250 contracts. A trader's long and short futures-equivalent positions are added to the trader's long and short futures positions to give "combined-long" and "combined-short" positions.*

Open interest, as reported to the Commission and as used in the COT *report, does not include open futures contracts against which notices of deliveries have been stopped by a trader or issued by the clearing organization of an exchange.*

Reportable Positions—*Clearing members, futures commission merchants, and foreign brokers (collectively called "reporting firms") file daily reports with the Commission. Those reports show the futures and option positions of traders that hold positions above specific reporting levels set by CFTC regulations. (Current Commission* *reporting levels can also be found at the Commission's website noted above.) If, at the daily market close, a reporting firm has a trader with a position at or above the Commission's reporting level in any single futures month or option expiration, it reports that trader's entire position in all futures and options expiration months in that commodity, regardless of size. The aggregate of all traders' positions reported to the Commission usually represents 70 to 90 percent of the total open interest in any given market. From time to time, the Commission will raise or lower the reporting levels in specific markets to strike a balance between collecting sufficient information to oversee the markets and minimizing the reporting burden on the futures industry.*

Commercial and Non-commercial Traders—*When an individual reportable trader is identified to the Commission, the trader is classified either as "commercial" or "non-commercial." All of a trader's reported futures positions in a commodity are classified as commercial if the trader uses futures contracts in that particular commodity for hedging as defined in the Commission's regulations (1.3(z)). A trading entity generally gets classified as a "commercial" by filing a statement with the Commission (on CFTC Form 40) that it is commercially ". . . engaged in business activities hedged by the use of the futures or option markets." In order to ensure that traders are classified with accuracy and consistency, the Commission staff may exercise judgment in re-classifying a trader if it has additional information about the trader's use of the markets.*

A trader may be classified as a commercial in some commodities and as a non-commercial in other commodities. A single trading entity cannot be classified as both a commercial and non-commercial in the same commodity. Nonetheless, a multi-functional organization that has more than one trading entity may have each trading entity classified separately in a commodity. For example, a financial organization trading in financial futures may have a banking entity whose positions are classified as commercial and have a separate money-management entity whose positions are classified as non-commercial.

Nonreportable Positions—*The long and short open interest shown as "Nonreportable Positions" are derived by subtracting total long and short "Reportable Positions" from the total open interest. Accordingly, for "Nonreportable Positions," the number of traders involved and the commercial/non-commercial classification of each trader are unknown.*

Spreading—*For the futures-only report, spreading measures the extent to which each non-commercial trader holds equal long and* *short futures positions. For the options-and-futures-combined report, spreading measures the extent to which each non-commercial trader holds equal combined-long and combined-short positions. For example, if a non-commercial trader in Eurodollar futures holds 2,000 long contracts and 1,500 short contracts, 500 contracts will appear in the "Long" category and 1,500 contracts will appear in the "Spreading" category. These figures do not include intermarket spreading, e.g., spreading Eurodollar futures against Treasury Note futures. [See a further explanation of "spreading" under the "Old and Other Futures" caption below.]*

Changes in Commitments from Previous Reports—*Changes represent the differences between the data for the current report date and the data published in the previous report.*

Percent of Open Interest—*Percents are calculated against the total open interest for the futures-only report and against the total futures-equivalent open interest for the options-and-futures-combined report. Percents less than 0.05 are shown as 0.0, and the percents may not add to exactly 100.0 due to rounding.*

Number of Traders—*To determine the total number of reportable traders in a market, a trader is counted only once regardless [of] whether the trader appears in more than one category (non-commercial traders may be long or short only and may be spreading; commercial traders may be long and short). To determine the number of traders in each category, however, a trader is counted in each category in which the trader holds a position. Therefore, the sum of the numbers of traders in each category will often exceed the "Total" number of traders in that market.*

Old and Other Futures *(long form only)—For selected commodities where there is a well-defined marketing season or crop year, the COT data are broken down by "old" and "other" crop years. [Table 2.2] lists those commodities and the first and last futures of the marketing season or crop year. In order not to disclose positions in a single future near its expiration, on the first business day of the month of the last future in an "old" crop year, the data for that last future are combined with the data for the next crop year and are shown as "old" crop futures. For example, in CBOT wheat, where the first month of the crop year is July and the last month of the prior crop year is May, on May 3, 2004, positions in the May 2004 futures month were aggregated with positions in the July 2004 through May 2005 futures months and shown as "old" crop futures—positions in all subsequent wheat futures months were shown as "other."*

TABLE 2.2 Major Markets for Which the COT Data Are Shown by Crop Year

Market*	First Future	Last Future
CBOT Wheat	July	May
CBOT Corn	December	September
CBOT Oats	July	May
CBOT Soybeans	September	August
CBOT Soybean Oil	October	September
CBOT Soybean Meal	October	September
CBOT Rough Rice	September	July
KCBT Wheat	July	May
MGE Wheat	September	July
CME Lean Hogs	December	October
CME Frozen Pork Bellies	February	August
NYBT Cocoa	December	September
NYBT Coffee C	December	September
NYBT Cotton No. 2	October	July
NYBT Frozen Concentrated Orange Juice	January	November

*CBOT: Chicago Board of Trade; KCBT: Kansas City Board of Trade; MGE: Minneapolis Grain Exchange; CME: Chicago Mercantile Exchange; NYBT: New York Board of Trade.

Source: Commodity Futures Trading Commission (www.cftc.gov).

> *For the "old" and "other" figures, spreading is calculated for equal long and short positions within a crop year. If a non-commercial trader holds a long position in an "old" crop-year future and an equal short position in an "other" crop-year future, the long position will be classified as "long-only" in the "old" crop year and the short position will be classified as "short-only" in the "other" crop year. In this example, in the "all" category, which considers each trader's positions without regard to crop year, that trader's positions will be classified as "spreading." For this reason, summing the "old" and "other" figures for long-only, for short-only, or for spreading will not necessarily equal the corresponding figure shown for "all" futures. Any differences result from traders that spread from an "old" crop-year future to an "other" crop-year future.*

Concentration Ratios (long form only)—The report shows the percents of open interest held by the largest four and eight reportable traders, without regard to whether they are classified as commercial or non-commercial. The concentration ratios are shown with trader positions computed on a gross long and gross short basis and on a net long or net short basis. The "Net Position" ratios are computed after offsetting each trader's equal long and short positions. Thus a re-

portable trader with relatively large, balanced long and short positions in a single market may be among the four and eight largest traders in both the gross long and gross short categories, but will probably not be included among the four and eight largest traders on a net basis.

Let's take a little deeper look at what the data is telling us by next looking at the COT report for wheat as of July 7, 2004 (see Table 2.3). What I want you to focus on will be the numbers under the "Commercial" heading. These are our buddies. In this case we see they were long 77,217 contracts and short 58,882 contracts. On balance they were long 18,335 more contracts than short. This tells us they were probably bullish, but one swallow does not make a summer, and one week's COT reading does not tell us to buy or sell.

In fact, we can see in the "changes" tabulation that the commercials reduced their long position by 4,178 contracts, more than they reduced their short position, which declined by 3,045. So, on the surface, while they still are net long, they were not adding to their positions on the long side this week, but actually cutting them back. They do hold 50.1 percent of all long contracts and 38.2 percent of all shorts.

We will begin looking at the commercials' position in several ways to understand how they accumulate and distribute when we want to hop aboard their freight train. One week's reading, on snapshot, does not show the entire picture, but this is where it all begins. To get a better view we will see how their buying increases over time and how it compares to the other players in the game.

The short form in Table 2.3 we just looked at leaves out one important player in the game: the public or nonreportable. The next tabulation

TABLE 2.3 Short Form from the CFTC

```
WHEAT - CHICAGO BOARD OF TRADE
FUTURES ONLY POSITIONS AS OF 07/27/04
------------------------------------------------------------------  NONREPORTABLE
     NON-COMMERCIAL        |    COMMERCIAL    |     TOTAL          POSITIONS
-----------------------------|--------------------|------------------|-------------------
 LONG  | SHORT  |SPREADS |  LONG  |  SHORT  | LONG  |  SHORT  | LONG   | SHORT
---------------------------------------------------------------------------------------
(CONTRACTS OF 5,000 BUSHELS)                        OPEN INTEREST:       154,277
COMMITMENTS
 35,655   53,872   13,699   77,217   58,882  126,571  126,453   27,706    27,824

CHANGES FROM 07/20/04 (CHANGE IN OPEN INTEREST:      -1,893)
   720    -1,279   -1,722   -4,178   -3,045   -5,180   -6,046    3,287     4,153

PERCENT OF OPEN INTEREST FOR EACH CATEGORY OF TRADERS
   23.1     34.9      8.9     50.1     38.2     82.0     82.0     18.0      18.0

NUMBER OF TRADERS IN EACH CATEGORY (TOTAL TRADERS:      248)
    66       91       51       62       58      159      180
```

Source: Commodity Futures Trading Commission (www.cftc.com).

(Table 2.4) is the complete long form, which allows us to look at the small speculators' weekly buying and selling numbers.

Our interest here is in the nonreportables, people who trade in such little amounts that the government is not worried about them influencing the markets. This group is the public, and on balance they lose money trading. This means we want to do the opposite of them in almost all instances. They are the great unwashed masses, uneducated to the ways of the markets. Emotions and rumors rule their trading strategies. We can key off this crowd by doing the opposite of what they do. In fact, when I show you how I use all this data to construct some market indicators you will see that the public, or small traders, usually do just about exactly the opposite of the commercials.

Note: Recently the CFTC made some changes in reporting requirements you should be aware of. Starting January 20, 2005, the CFTC made changes in what they attribute to the large trader positions. The intent of these guys has been to have from 75 percent to 90 percent of open interest

TABLE 2.4 Long Form from the CFTC

```
Commitments of Traders - Futures Only, July 27, 2004
-------------------------
        :   Total  :                      Reportable Positions
    :  Nonreportable
    :--------------------------------------------------------------------------
 ----- :     Positions
        :   Open   :       Non-Commercial      :      Commercial      :      Total
    :
    :  Interest :  Long   :  Short   : Spreading:  Long  :  Short   :  Long   :
 Short   :   Long  :  Short
-----------------------------------------------------------------------------------
-------------------------
        :          :  (CONTRACTS OF 5,000 BUSHELS)
    :
        :          :
    :
 All  :   154,277:    35,655     53,872     13,699     77,217     58,882    126,571
 126,453:    27,706     27,824
 Old  :   151,673:    36,166     54,078     12,732     75,478     57,902    124,376
 124,712:    27,297     26,961
 Other:     2,604:       427        732         29      1,739        980      2,195
 1,741:       409        863
    :
        :          :           Changes in Commitments from: July 20, 2004
    :
        :   -1,893:       720     -1,279     -1,722     -4,178     -3,045     -5,180     -
 6,046:     3,287     4,153
    :
        :          :  Percent of Open Interest Represented by Each Category of Trader
    :
 All  :    100.0:       23.1       34.9        8.9       50.1       38.2       82.0
 82.0:      18.0       18.0
 Old  :    100.0:       23.8       35.7        8.4       49.8       38.2       82.0
 82.2:      18.0       17.8
 Other:    100.0:       16.4       28.1        1.1       66.8       37.6       84.3
 66.9:      15.7       33.1
    :
        :# Traders :             Number of Traders in Each Category
    :
 All  :      248:        66         91         51         62         58        159
 180:
 Old  :      247:        69         92         48         61         57        158
 176:
 Other:       57:         7          8          2         11         32         19
 42:
```

Source: Commodity Futures Trading Commission (www.cftc.gov).

be represented by large trader positions. Thus from time to time as overall open interest increases and decreases they adjust the sizes of positions that need to be reported.

The last previous change in these figures took place in May of 2000, so, as you can see, these are not changes that come and go every week. The largest of the recent changes came in the S&P E-Mini reporting requirements, where the old definition of a large trader was 300 contracts and the number now steps up to 1,000. I'm certain you will hear of these changes, and I see no reason why they will affect the impact this data has on the markets. Table 2.5 shows the step-up in large trader reporting.

TABLE 2.5 Large Trader Reporting

Commodity	Previous Level	Level Starting January 20, 2005
Agricultural		
Wheat	100	150
Corn	150	250
Soybeans	100	150
Cotton	50	100
Sugar No. 11	400	500
Milk, Class 3	25	50
Natural Resources		
Natural Gas	175	200
Crude Oil, Sweet—No. 2 Heating Oil Crack Spread	25	250
Crude Oil, Sweet—Unleaded Gasoline Crack Spread	25	150
Unleaded Gasoline—No. 2 Heating Oil Spread Swap	25	150
Financial		
30-Year U.S. Treasury Bonds	1,000	1,500
10-Year U.S. Treasury Notes	1,000	2,000
5-Year U.S. Treasury Notes	800	2,000
2-Year U.S. Treasury Notes	500	1,000
3-Month Eurodollars Rates	1,000	3,000
30-Day Fed Funds	300	600
1-Month LIBOR Rates	300	600
E-Mini S&P 500 Stock Price Index	300	1,000
S&P 400 MidCap Stock Index	100	200
Dow Jones Industrial Average	100	200
Nasdaq-100 Stock Index	100	200
Russell 2000 Stock Index	100	200
NIKKEI Stock Index	100	200

Effective for large trader data dated January 20, 2005, and later. The first commitment reports using the new levels are dated January 25, 2005. Reporting levels for commodities not listed are unchanged.

Source: Commodity futures Trading Commission (www.cftc.gov).

OUR WORK HAS JUST BEGUN

By now you know where and how to access what the insiders (and outsiders) are doing. But this is really only the tip of the iceberg, as just looking at the reports will not tell you much. I have found that it is best to put their buying and selling into perspective, so that we can get a feel for exactly when they are really bullish or bearish on a market.

Want to know how I do that? Good, just keep reading. . . .

CHAPTER 3

Understanding the Commercials

A Record of Their Buying and Selling

Timing has a lot to do with the success of a rain dance.

—Old Indian adage

Now that you understand who the commercials are, I want to show you the history of their actual buying and selling over the past 20 years so you can begin not only to learn their trading or investing style but also to better understand how these guys and gals operate in the marketplace.

The most common assumption is that if the commercials go net long (they have more contracts on the buy side than the sell side), prices will rally. This, as you will see, is not quite the case. Commercial buying and selling is not like a light switch that gets turned on and then markets immediately rally. Far from it—there is a subtle nuance to understanding the commercials and how to profit from them. In Chapter 4 I explain my favorite indicator to focus on their activity. Until you understand the basic way they accumulate and distribute, you will be confused. That's the purpose of this chapter—no, not to confuse you, but to make certain you are fully cognizant of how the commercials enter and exit the markets.

It took me many years to appreciate and understand the subtleties of this esteemed group of speculators. My job, in this book, is to transfer as much of the knowledge to you as possible in the shortest period of time. I learned what I did by looking at charts—chart after chart, in fact, so I have a few for you to cut your teeth on.

WHEAT 1992–1998

The chart of wheat (see Figure 3.1) is typical of commercial activity. You will see this time and time again. Wheat may well be the most singularly used commodity on the planet. As bread is the staff of life, wheat has been actively traded for hundreds of years and has many lessons to teach us. First, let me explain what you are looking at in the chart. The top of the chart is a weekly record of how wheat has traded. This is a continuous record representing how all wheat contracts have traded. I prefer using weekly charts for several reasons: we get the information once a week, not on a daily time frame. There is less data to follow. I like to keep it simple, and these simple weekly charts are what I have always used. Monthly charts are okay, but often are late in telling us when the commercial traders have gone heavily long or short.

The window below the price action is the actual net difference between the long and short positions these people have. In other words, we take the number of long contracts they have and subtract the total number of short contracts. By doing this we arrive at the "net position," which will be net long or net short. The horizontal zero line represents when buying and selling totals are equal: the commercials have the same number of longs as they do shorts. When the net position is above the zero line the commercials have more longs than shorts; when it is below this line they have more sales on than they do long positions. If you go ahead and take a

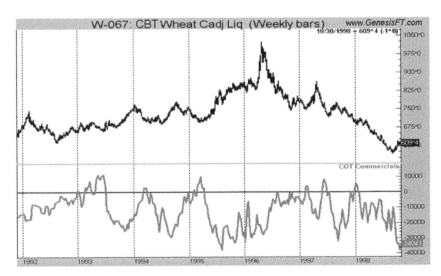

FIGURE 3.1 Buying Exceeded Selling for the Commercials
Source: Genesis Financial Technologies, Inc. (www.GenesisFT.com).

look at the chart, you should first be struck with the fact the commercials were short most all the time; in fact, there were only six instances in this entire seven-year window of market activity where they were net long!

As you recall from Chapter 2, though, these guys are hedgers and are usually selling. As you can now see, it is very unusual for them to be long for an extended period of time. This does vary from market to market, but as a general rule they tend to do more selling than buying, and in many markets, as you will see, they have never been net long.

This leads us to several interesting market insights. First, just because the commercials went net short does not mean a market is going to decline. They do not use the markets for speculation. They use the markets to buy and sell product they need when they do or do not need it.

Second, notice in Figure 3.1 that every time the commercials' buying exceeded their selling and the net position got above the zero line, a market rally was not far away.

I'll bet you are asking yourself some questions just about now and have also made an astute observation.

The common question is, how can a market rally so much when the commercials are selling? The answer is they are selling product they own. They are not trying to make money *from* the market by selling short; rather, they are selling what they own *to* the marketplace. This means the commercials own the wheat, from their production, and are selling it so they are actually taking a profit. They are not trying to put the market down; they are liquidating and taking profits, saying they will deliver their wheat when the contract expires. Never forget the commercials do not make money from buying and selling in the market; they are hedgers, using the market to sell what they own or buy what they want to own.

An Astute Observation

The astute observation is that it seems to be the extremes that matter more than the crossovers from bullish to bearish or anything else. Bingo! That is exactly what we will be looking for: extreme levels of bullishness or bearishness to help us spot tops and bottoms—major points to get long or short. Then, even then, the commercials show us the zone they take action in. They do not say, "Okay, everyone, listen up—today is the day to sell." Far from it; we will use other tools for timing our entries once the zones have been established.

Figure 3.2 is the exact same as what you just looked at, except I have added dashed lines to show the extremes of commercial buying and selling. Now Figure 3.1 makes more sense and drives home the importance of waiting for these guys to become extreme in their position.

Also notice how it does not take much buying—much time above the

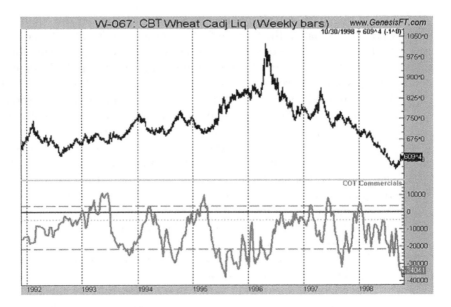

FIGURE 3.2 Extremes of Commercial Buying and Selling
Source: Genesis Financial Technologies, Inc. (www.GenesisFT.com).

zero line—to trigger a rally, nor does it take very positive readings to ignite rallies, while it takes a lot of selling—a larger dip below the zero line than above—to set the stage for a decline. This is due to the fact, as pointed out earlier, that they are usually sellers, so we need greater amounts of selling and less of buying to establish our view of the markets.

GOLD 1999–2004

Figure 3.3 shows this to be true of gold. The commercials were net short as early as 2002, yet the market did not plunge. That greatly confused many followers of this information, but not you and me, as we know it is the extremes we look for. Indeed, the major decline of gold in 2004 began with a historically large amount of selling by this smart money crowd. I admonish you to keep this point in mind: it is the extremely bullish or bearish stances the commercials make that tip us as to what to do. If they have just begun more selling than buying, unless that is an extreme level, it means very little to us.

The commercials at this point were doing more selling than at any time in the prior six years!

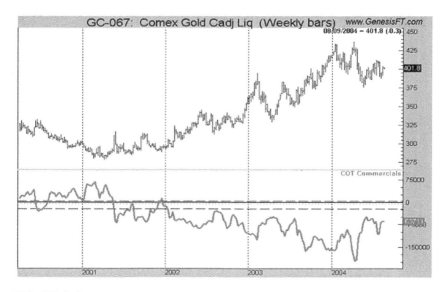

FIGURE 3.3 Gold Chart
Source: Genesis Financial Technologies, Inc. (www.GenesisFT.com).

COFFEE 1987–1993

The long-term chart of coffee (see Figure 3.4) teaches the same lesson: it is the extremes in commercial selling that set up the best sell points as well as the extremes in buying, and we should not expect the extreme buying levels to be as far above the zero line as the extreme selling levels are below it. That's the lesson to learn!

As you can see in Figure 3.4, the commercials were net short—they had more sells than longs—from 1987 through 1993 with the exception of one brief move to the long side—and an extreme—at the end of 1990. That coincided with one of the few rallies in this market during this seven-year window.

AND A LESSON TO RELEARN WITH A VIEW OF THE STOCK MARKET

Figure 3.5 shows you the S&P 500, the best measure of United States stock prices. The lesson you just learned was that extremely high readings are bullish and extremely low readings are bearish. With that in mind, check out the chart and you will see what a brilliant record these guys had

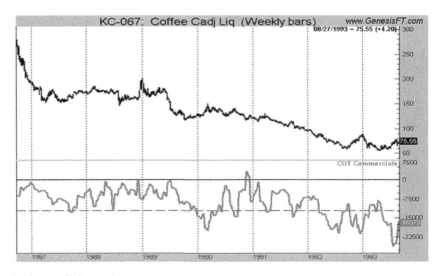

FIGURE 3.4 Coffee Chart
Source: Genesis Financial Technologies, Inc. (www.GenesisFT.com).

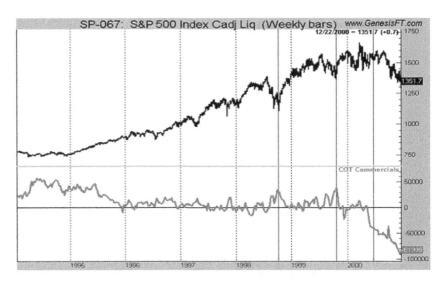

FIGURE 3.5 S&P 500 Index Chart
Source: Genesis Financial Technologies, Inc. (www.GenesisFT.com).

in showing us the buy points in the fall of 1998 and 1999 when their buying reached historically high levels, higher than seen in the prior five years. Boy, these guys were big buyers.

Their selling was equally fortuitous. Check out the massive amount of selling we see at the start of 2000 when the largest bear market in 70 years began. At that time the commercials had taken on the largest short position in the S&P 500 index in the history of the data! In 18 years they had never been this bearish. Stocks plummeted in response, and these insiders must have made hundreds of millions of dollars from correctly calling this critical market turning point. It is the excessive position of the commercials that gets us excited—the extreme reading of bullishness or bearishness that has the strongest and most reliable forecasting power.

In Retrospect

Pundits, in retrospect, have said the crash was caused by a whole host of things. Some say it was the decline of the Clinton presidency, the end of high tech, extreme market valuations, cyclical phenomena, and on and on. Whatever the real reason is does not matter and is not of much use to the speculator. What we want is something that at the time tells us to pitch our stocks. The commercials did just that.

What we have seen gives rise to a rule. What we have seen is that there is money to be made by aligning ourselves with this crowd when they are extremely bullish or bearish.

LESSON ONE IN USING THE COMMERCIAL DATA

Multiyear highs in net buying beget bull markets. Multiyear lows in net selling beget bear markets.

That's about as simple as it gets. When you see the highest level for years in commercial buying, expect a dramatic up move to soon unfold (and vice versa). Note that the index need not stay at the extreme bullish/bearish reading, and in fact often the commercials abandon the excessive reading as the trend move unfolds. I'd counsel you to not expect them to stay at the extreme reading for long, because once they get these massive positions on they begin working them off in their hedging operations.

Remember that we don't want just a little excess buying or selling. We want a massive amount, and we want it to be at historical levels. The most buying/selling for the last four years is a pretty good rule of thumb to demand from our monitoring of the commercials' flow of money.

BRITISH POUND AND EXCESSIVE BUYING/SELLING

We began with agricultural or natural resource commodities, shifted to stocks, and will now take a peek at the British pound, a man-made or synthetic commodity. As shown in Figure 3.6, in mid-1999 the index of the commercials' net position hit a historically high level, the highest amount of net buying done in the past 14 years. The commercials were buying everything in sight, suggesting that we might want to listen up and join them in the pursuit of a bull market.

What happened is an interesting story in the art of speculating. Prices rallied, as they should, presenting traders with a move of more than $8,000 to attempt to take advantage of. I assume, in some fashion, even the most inexperienced trader could have captured part of this move.

That is, until a scant 26 weeks later the commercials reversed themselves with heavy selling. The net position swung to the lowest level in 10 years, clearly telling us that the big guys were selling, selling, selling in preparation for a market slide. My point is that we need to continually monitor what this camp is doing. They can and will spin on a dime, going from very bullish to very bearish as they assess the situation and respond

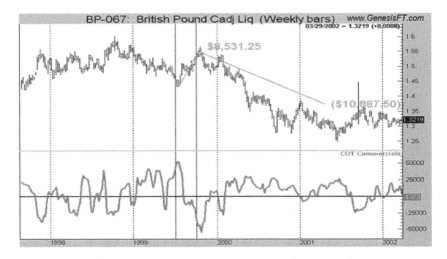

FIGURE 3.6 British Pound Chart
Source: Genesis Financial Technologies, Inc. (www.GenesisFT.com).

to market-driven conditions, not their mere belief of what the market will do. In this case their selling set up an opportunity for the average guy and gal to take advantage of a market downdraft with the potential for more than $12,000 profits.

This was a pretty picture painted by our good friends, and painted in the crisp style of Norman Rockwell, not the impressionistic strokes of Paul Cezanne. Each time they moved to an extreme level, which we can identify here as a multiyear new high or new low, the stage was set for us to enter the play. After acts one and two were completed, the climax where the good guys win in act three is our cue to come to center stage.

CHAPTER 4

The COT Index

Now comes a method to quantify the actions of the commercials.

As the preceding chapter showed, the markets are not total madness. Things happen for a reason, and, by and large, that driving force is the commercials' attitude toward a market as expressed by their actual buying and selling. In this chapter I will be introducing the first way to quantify and stabilize the weekly readings of the commercials so that we have a consistent reference point by which to judge their actions.

The multiyear highs and lows work quite well in spotting major tops and bottoms. However, if we normalize the information by making an index or indicator of the commercials' buying and selling, there are more opportunities, and more concise ones at that. This can be accomplished by the wonders of mathematics. The formula is simple and direct.

I am not sure who first began looking at the "Commitments of Traders" (COT) data in this fashion. Perhaps it was Steve Briese, a consummate and brilliant follower of the information, or Joe Van Nice, a trader good enough to cash out to a ranch in Montana. If it wasn't one of them, then it was me, I guess, as I have been looking at this data longer than anyone. What we, or they, did was compare the current week's level of the net long/short position to where it had been over the prior three years. Poised in this fashion we can actually arrive at an index that shows the percentage of bullishness being expressed by this week's reading against all readings of the last three years. For now I will use this three-year time frame as that seems to be the one most services have come to use, though, as you shall see, it has limitations.

The equation looks like this:

$$\frac{(\text{Current week's value} - \text{Lowest value of last three years})}{(\text{Highest high of last three years} - \text{Lowest low of last three years})} \times 100$$

For example:

Current week's value	350
Lowest value of last three years	−150
Difference	200
Highest high of last three years	750
Lowest low of last three years	−150
Difference	600

This week's value is:

$$(200 \div 600) \times 100 = 0.33 \times 100 = 33\%$$

What this equation does is place the current week's reading into perspective of the last three years of commercials' buying and selling. The higher the percentage, above 80 percent, the more buying they have done (i.e., the more bullish they are). By the same token, when the index is low, usually below 20 percent, they have not been doing much buying; we can then conclude that they are facing the market with a negative bias. These are very good reference points: above 80 percent the market should rally, and below 20 percent it should decline.

Please notice I did not say *when* the market should rally. The index is not a timing tool for the most part.

The formula provides insight into the commercials that may not be seen at a glance or upon first blush. Here's an example of how it helps us monitor the relative bullish position these guys have been taking. Picture, if you will, this situation: the commercials are net long at this week's reading (they have purchased more than they have sold).

Sounds bullish. But it may not indicate a strong bullishness, which is where the importance of perspective comes into play. Consider a scenario where the commercials are net long 1,000 contracts. The most net long they have been in the past three years has been 9,200 contracts, and the least net long they have been is 500 contracts.

I note, in this example, that they are net long. But the size of their long position is small, 1,000 longs, compared to the greatest long position they have had in the past three years of 9,200 contracts. The math is: 1,000 minus 500 equaling 500, that result divided by the extreme figures of 9,200 minus 500 or 8,700. The step of 500 divided by 8,700 tells us that the relative position this week for the commercials' percentage of bullishness is at 5.7 percent! Yes, they are net long, but compared to the past three years they are carrying a very small long position. This infers that they are at a very low level of bullishness relative to their positions over the past three years.

SO MUCH FOR THEORY

Let's turn our attention to some real data to see how the index works in conjunction with the net index of longs and shorts. Figure 4.1, a chart of gold, makes my point. While the commercials were net short this market in mid-2004, the COT index (bottom panel) had moved up from 0 percent bullish, rising to 69 percent bullish in May of that year. A rally quickly followed—despite the fact the commercials were net short. The absolute position they had was not nearly as important as how the current week's reading fit into the grand scheme of what they had been doing.

As you can see, despite being net short, this was the most bullish reading in the COT data for more than three years, when in January 2001 the index was also at high levels. Ahhh . . . so much of life is relative. When I lived in Montana a warm day in March was above 50 degrees

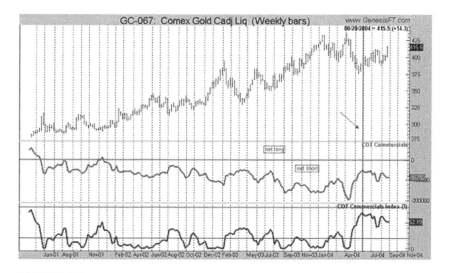

FIGURE 4.1 Gold Chart
Source: Genesis Financial Technologies, Inc. (www.GenesisFT.com).

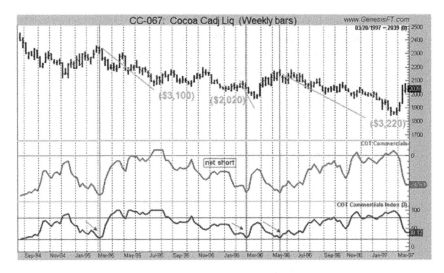

FIGURE 4.2   Cocoa Chart
Source: Genesis Financial Technologies, Inc. (www.GenesisFT.com).

Fahrenheit. Now, living in St. Croix, a warm day in March is anything above 85!

Next we will look at Figure 4.2, a chart of cocoa in 1996–1997 when the commercials had been net short the entire time. Does that mean we should just mortgage the farm and sell short? I don't think so! What it means is that we should wait until this selling becomes extreme, and then look for our sell point. I have marked off such points on Figure 4.2 as well as the potential dollars to be made from selling short at these times.

When you consider that the margin, or amount you would have to have put up to make the bet, in this case was less than $1,500, you can get a sense of the possibilities that present themselves for followers of what the commercials buy and sell.

A COMMERCIALS' VIEW OF THE BRITISH POUND

The British pound is an actively traded market, by the public as well as by the commercials. Figure 4.3 is a weekly chart showing how the commercials have approached this market for the past four years. The key point to keep in mind is that readings greater than 75 on the index can

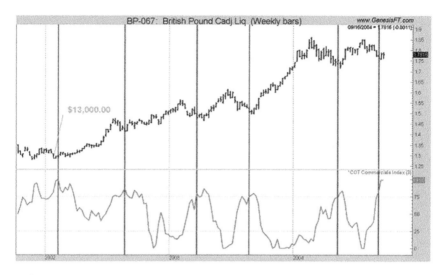

FIGURE 4.3 British Pound Chart
Source: Genesis Financial Technologies, Inc. (www.GenesisFT.com).

mean only one thing: on a relative basis the commercials have been doing 75 percent more buying now compared to the past three years. Such readings are often, not always but often enough, found at market low points.

To prove this, just take a peek at the pound to see if that does not hold true—that high levels in the index spot very good buying points.

BULLISH ON CRUDE OIL

It should come as no great shock, then, that when the commercials became heavily long on crude oil it also staged some very profitable rallies (see Figure 4.4). The energy scare of 2004 was heralded by a great deal of buying by commercials in the middle of 2003 when the COT index rose to 100 percent, telling us that this was the most bullish on crude oil they had been in three years.

They do not get that bullish for no reason at all. These are smart cookies. They get bullish because they know something, and they want to make some money from that inside commercial information. What could have been a cleaner and more clear-cut signal of the intentions of the professionals than such a bullish reading? They told us, or at least those of us who read the COT data, what they were doing. Sure, they did not ring a bell or send an e-mail; they just reported it to the government. It is our responsibility to read, decipher, and decide.

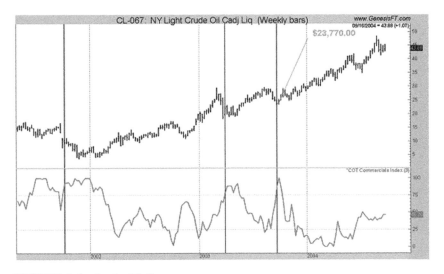

FIGURE 4.4 Crude Oil Chart
Source: Genesis Financial Technologies, Inc. (www.GenesisFT.com).

THE SILVER BULLS AND THE COT

Another example would be silver. During the entire time period on the chart in Figure 4.5 the commercials had been short silver. But, as they prove to us in this example, it is not the absolute position that matters. Far from it. It is the relative position over the time period under observation, in this case three years, that matters the most.

If you don't know it now, you soon will. There are camps or sides in most markets, and nowhere else are they more apparent than in the precious metals, gold and silver. The bullish camp, those looking for wildly higher prices, has made a mantra and religion out of silver. To them the world is going to hell and the sooner the better. I feel that way myself at times, but there are other moments when I know life will move forward and things will get better.

The silver bulls have, for years, misused and misunderstood the COT data. They have chided the commercials for being short, and chided them for seemingly not buying at the lows, as they have been net short for years. In fact, the commercials have been net short since 1984 (see Figure 4.6). The silver bulls spin an enticing story of a world with no more silver. Over and over they claim, "There are only about 24 silver mines in the

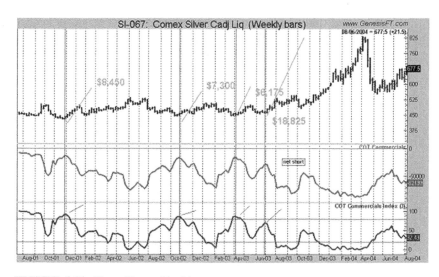

FIGURE 4.5 Silver Chart—Weekly
Source: Genesis Financial Technologies, Inc. (www.GenesisFT.com).

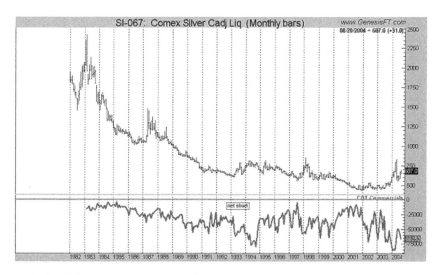

FIGURE 4.6 Silver Chart—Monthly
Source: Genesis Financial Technologies, Inc. (www.GenesisFT.com).

world, and that small amount of production can't possibly keep up with current silver needs." If you don't like that line of reasoning they have others. But does it matter, really matter? I don't think so. Stories are stories. Commercials plunking down millions of dollars of real money means a great deal more to me than some guy writing a market letter out of his basement.

Knowing as we do that the commercials use the market for their business purposes, we can understand what's going on here. They have used the market—used the silver bulls—to hedge production and consumption. It is a fair statement to say they have snookered the silver zealots into providing the buyers and sellers they need for their business.

When it comes down to which camp to bet with, no doubt about it, the true believers will lose every time to the professionals. That's the sure bet.

In retrospect, considering the price of silver has yet to take off, the commercials have done the right thing—they have sold inventory into the rallies. Every time they have taken on a large short position, in fact, the price of silver has come down. Hey, I told you these guys are no dummies. Just consider that for 22 years the money has been made selling into the rallies or staying short. For 22 years the commercials have never been net long in silver, never, not even for one week!

So let me tell you this:

If you ever see the commercials go net long silver, look for a major bull market.

Amen, brother. That will be the time to join the church, to heap praises upon the altar of silver, to sing and shout and jump about, like Little Richard, Jerry Lee Lewis, or William Jennings Bryan, singing the old-time silver revival song. Until then, though, when the commercials are relatively bullish, look to buy long and when relatively bearish be willing to take sell signals. They may well be net short, but if that short position is small as a percentage of recent activity, they are telling us to hop to the long side. The markets are not about a religion or a belief system; they are about commercial enterprise, which is best represented by the buying and selling of the trade, the insiders of this great financial game. America, what a great place! Through this book I will present you with examples of using the commercial data to understand market moves. You can catch real time examples on my website www.ireallytrade.com. Check out Larry Live and you will see that I trade using the commercials' data on a regular basis.

I'll get back to the commercials and an even better way of following them. But right now I'd like to show you . . .

CHAPTER 5

For Every Insider There Is an Outsider

One man's pain is another man's gain.

The old comment that God must love poor people because he made so many of them is a fitting reference to stock and commodity traders. I have seen estimates stating that as many as 90 percent of public traders lose money trading, down to what I think is more accurate—that about 80 percent of public traders are net losers.

To me that's just great news—they have to lose that money to someone, hopefully me. It is also bad news—I don't exactly take pleasure in others' financial demise. But it needn't be that way. If the great unwashed masses would just study, learn, and buy a book or two (as you have), they would greatly enhance their ability to walk away winners. Instead they take tips from brokers, bankers, brothers-in-law, barbers, and babes. That's just so dumb.

Want to see how dumb that is? I'll show you. Once a week, along with the "Commitments of Traders" (COT) report, the government guys also give us the net long/short position of small traders, "others" in their report. In this fashion we can see what the public is doing and see how right or wrong they are about the markets. Figure 5.1 reflects weekly prices of the commodity in question, and underneath the price area you can see (in the "COT Small Spec" area) the net position of the little guys, short subtracted from long. Look for the bold horizontal zero line on the chart in Figure 5.1 to see their net long/short position.

What you will see is a real eye-opener as to what *we*, guys and gals like you and me, do until we learn how this game is played. I am not saying that all small speculators lose money. What I am saying is that until

41

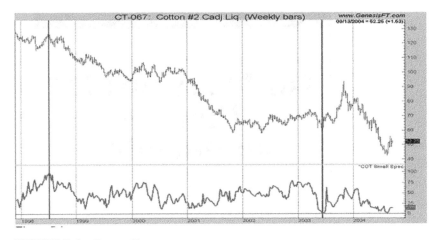

FIGURE 5.1   Cotton Chart
Source: Genesis Financial Technologies, Inc. (www.GenesisFT.com).

they wake up and learn the lessons of this business they will most likely be perpetual losers.

Figure 5.1 is a chart of cotton from 1998 forward. During this entire massive bear market and slide in cotton prices, the public was net long (the index line is above the zero line). There are two very important points to look at before you can begin to understand how these guys act and react toward price movement.

LARGEST NET LONG POSITION

As the actual record of the small speculators' buying and selling shows, they held the largest number of net long contracts on July 3, 1998, the exact start of a six-and-a-half-year relentless erosion of prices in this market.

SMALLEST NET LONG POSITION

Again, as the actual record shows (I don't make up these numbers), the most bearish they were was the June 6, 2003, low in cotton when they had actually gone slightly net short—right at the start of the largest up move of the six years! They missed the sell at the highs and failed to be buyers at the lows. This is typical of what the public does, year in and year out, in the majority of the markets, the majority of the time. By the way, had you sold one contract on 1998 when they were such heavy buyers you could have made close to $32,000 on your $500 investment. That is if you had sold short, if you had rolled the position, and if you exited close to the low. Yes, there are lots of ifs there, and for a reason. But you can see the potential profits in fading the public.

If we had decided to buy long when they became net sellers in 2003, there was an opportunity to make about $16,000 on the ensuing up move. Would you have captured all of it? Probably not, but I'd like to think that you could have captured a chunk of it. The point of all this is to illustrate how wrong this crowd is. This means, though, that we can use them as a contrarian indicator to help us predict the markets and also as a strong warning that we cannot react to markets in the fashion that seems natural, as that is the fashion in which the public operates. Their trading record is a stark warning to us that, unless we mend our ways, we will be in the boat they are in, a boat destined to sink upon the high seas of finance.

BEATING THE MARKET WITH THE BRITISH POUND

Let's turn our attention from cotton to a currency, the British pound in Figure 5.2. Could it be that public currency players trade in a different manner than cotton speculators? It is certainly possible. After all, we have

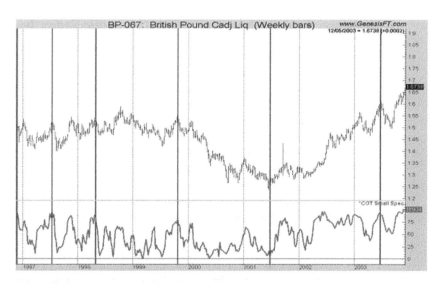

FIGURE 5.2 British Pound Chart
Source: Genesis Financial Technologies, Inc. (www.GenesisFT.com).

two entirely different markets here—one trading a real commodity and
the other trading a currency with no planting, growing, or harvest season.
During this seven-year window we see that small speculators were net
long the entire time. We know that just being net long or short is not what
we are looking for. No. What we follow is how bullish (a high reading) or
bearish (a low reading) they are.

Many people have looked at this data, looking at just the net position.
Their thinking has been that when the public goes net short, buy. When
the public goes net long, sell. That is not the answer to applying this data.
The answer and insight into the market will come from noting the relative
changes in the small speculators' positions and the times when they are
extreme in their investment position.

As one example in the British pound chart, Figure 5.2, we see one of
their most extreme bearish views, the lowest reading in the net position. It
came at the June 2001 low point. The extreme highs were not far away
from some excellent sell points. This is not atypical behavior. It is the way
these people play the market, year in and year out, as they have not yet
learned the rules of my game.

FIRST RULE FOR THE PUBLIC INDEX

*Look to sell short when the public is at extremely high levels of
bullishness. Look to buy long when the public index is at extremely low levels of bullishness.*

Please notice that just about every one of the best buy points came
when the public's net position line had dipped, telling us they were doing
more selling than buying. Time after time (as I have marked) when the
line declined, as they had stepped up their selling, prices rallied. In fact, I
cannot find *any* strong buy points where the public stepped in as aggressive buyers.

No wonder so many of them lose so much of the time. Their instinc-
tual behavior is to buy at market highs and sell at market lows. This psy-
che exists in all of us. You have to reprogram yourself to avoid buying
after a market has had a large, emotionally attractive up move. You have a
choice to invest and trade with your natural responses—the same as the
public shown here—or relearn how to respond to market action. The
choice is yours!

This gives rise to the next rule for using this data. This rule is
about the alignment with the "right forces" in the world of finance. Here it is.

SECOND RULE FOR THE PUBLIC INDEX

Learn to do the exact opposite of public traders as a group. When they are sellers, look to buy long. When they have been buyers, look to sell short.

GOLD DOES NOT ALWAYS GLITTER

The chart of gold in Figure 5.3 may help you understand why we do not want to follow this crowd, but instead we want to buck them by doing the opposite. There were some huge declines in this market in the 1995 to 2001 time period. Every time—yes, every time—the public stepped up their buying, the index rose to a high level and gold collapsed. It is almost as though there is some force that propels the public into buying at exactly the wrong times. I have certainly had that urge as well, and if you have traded much I'm certain we have that in common. Some emotional twitch makes us buy right at a market high.

To me this is a lot like fly-fishing for trout. I'd like you to join me on my favorite fishing stream in my home state of Montana. I have few secrets in life, but the exact location of that stream is more valuable than

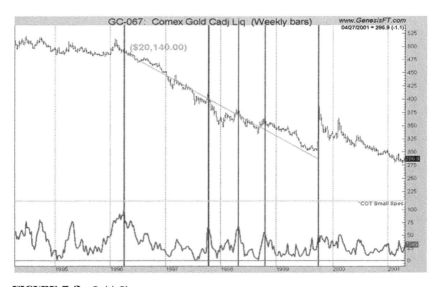

FIGURE 5.3 Gold Chart
Source: Genesis Financial Technologies, Inc. (www.GenesisFT.com).

gold. If you were there with me on a warm August evening, we'd cast my favorite fly (an irritable) at the head of some riffles, keeping an eye on the fly as it almost dances on the water, just letting it drift to where we begin to haul in for a recast.

No fish on our first cast.

So we cast again. This time I see a big brown trout gingerly approach the fly. What do I do? Do I let the fly just float there? No way! I tweak it ever so lightly, moving it just a little bit away from the fish. He darts back, takes another long hard look at my little fluff of deer hair skimming along on the surface. Seeing that, I know I'm just about to catch him. I twitch the fly one more time, taking it away from him—yes, *away*.

Whap! He strikes and I set the hook. I got him! That lunker of a brown fell for my trap. He just couldn't take it any longer, the twitching, the removal of the apparent morsel. Giving him no time to think any longer is what got him into my frying pan.

Stock and commodity prices do the same thing to you and me. They tantalize us, trick us, tease us. And just when we can't stand it any longer, we are hooked and reeled into the frying pan.

That is the honest to God's truth of what happens to us as traders/investors. Until you learn not to fall for that twitch and tease gambit you will never walk away a winner.

In many ways, looking at the weekly report of public buying/selling is like watching fish getting hooked. When the public is biting, keep your mouth closed.

SOYBEAN SOLILOQUY

Let's take one more look at these amusing phenomena of the public doing the wrong thing at the wrong time, like lemmings running into the sea. This time the sea is a weekly chart of soybeans (Figure 5.4). I have marked off the extreme highs where the small speculators were buying, and the extreme lows where they were selling.

In the fall of 2003 the public shied away from soybeans with the most bearish view, the least buying, since 1999. Despite the uptrend in beans, they were persistent in their unwillingness to enter the long side of this market. Too bad for them, as this market began a skyrocketing move with the potential to turn every $1,000 you plunked down into $27,000.

As a general rule of life, I have learned that whatever the masses do, most of the time it is the wrong thing to do. The majority is just that: the majority. The majority is not right in most instances. Look no further than

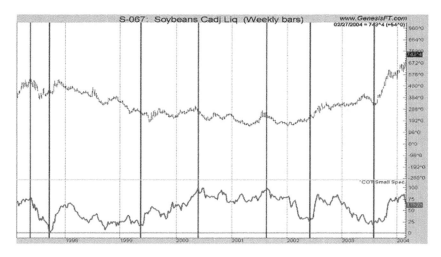

FIGURE 5.4 Soybeans Chart
Source: Genesis Financial Technologies, Inc. (www.GenesisFT.com).

the White House, our government of the majority, or the tax codes for further proof.

There is seldom any wisdom in a consensus viewpoint. The markets know all and reveal all of life's lessons and adages. It has proven this to me, time and again. Here are a few more charts for your study. They were chosen at random to illustrate the two rules given in this chapter (see Figures 5.5, 5.6, and 5.7).

Now that you have learned the basics of what makes the fish bite, I'd like to show you a practical way of using this information. It's quite simple. We do the same thing we did with the commercials' positions, where we converted the net index into an indicator covering the last three years' wanderings on our charts. The formula is exactly the same as in the prior chapter; just use the small traders' numbers, not the commercials'.

USING THE INDEX, NOT JUST THE NET LONG POSITION

Let's revisit the lumber chart we just looked at but this time with the three-year look-back index (see Figure 5.8). I have marked off with heavier vertical lines every time the public index rose above 75 percent. The smallest of the down moves could have turned your $1,500 into almost $9,000 had you had the wisdom and foresight to sell in February 2003. If you are like most of my readers, you probably did not even know that

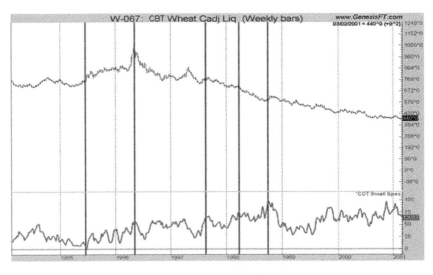

FIGURE 5.5 Wheat Chart
Source: Genesis Financial Technologies, Inc. (www.GenesisFT.com).

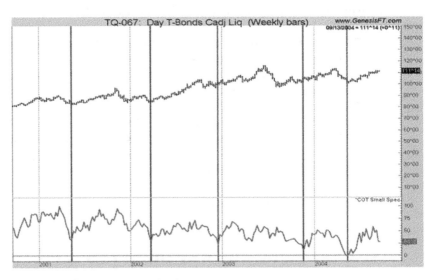

FIGURE 5.6 Treasury Bonds Chart
Source: Genesis Financial Technologies, Inc. (www.GenesisFT.com).

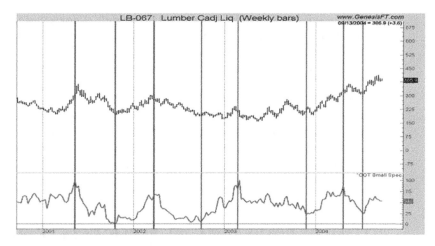

FIGURE 5.7 Lumber Chart
Source: Genesis Financial Technologies, Inc. (www.GenesisFT.com).

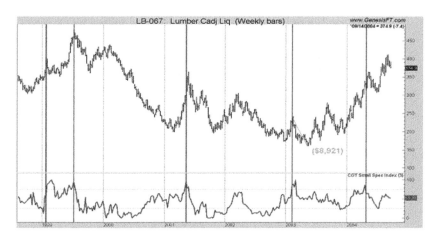

FIGURE 5.8 Lumber Weekly Chart with COT Index
Source: Genesis Financial Technologies, Inc. (www.GenesisFT.com).

lumber traded, just like gold, wheat, and corn. Well, it does, and it is driven by market forces just like all other markets. One important force is that when the public becomes too bullish, this index rising above 75 percent, a market slide and a short selling opportunity are not far away.

There is a problem here, though. While the sell signals were pretty much on the button, the really low levels of public buying (the index falling below 25 percent) did not always produce a market rally. Although the low reading in late 2003 and mid-2004, where the bearish view of the public produced great rallies for us to attempt to ride, may suggest buy signals, study the chart and you will see many instances where it would not have been a good time to buy.

BULLISH ON BONDS WHEN THE PUBLIC GETS BEARISH

I'd like to take you through a few more charts to get you up to speed on how to use the public. Our next chart to study is of bonds from 2000 to 2004 (see Figure 5.9). With one exception, every time the public became bearish on bonds, bonds rallied, and often by quite a bit. Notice the mid-2001 rally where a $3,000 investment, the margin in bonds at that time, could have made a hefty $14,656 for you in a little over 30 weeks. Had you plunked down $30,000, you stood to make $146,560 on just this one run.

How can this be? Why does it happen? Is the public destined for continual market failure? All good questions. It is true, sad but true, that the

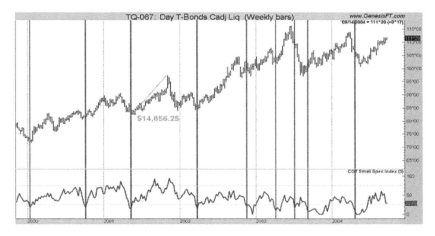

FIGURE 5.9 Treasury Bonds Chart
Source: Genesis Financial Technologies, Inc. (www.GenesisFT.com).

public buys at more highs than lows. If you are to become successful at all this, you need to understand why it happens so you do not commit the same folly. It happens, I think, for three primary reasons:

1. Risking money is a very emotional decision.
2. The public does not know the rules of the game.
3. Emotions win over logic.

It's tough to pull money out of your pocket and plunk it down on some speculative venture that has a high chance of failure, despite the fact that if you are correct you may make 5 to 10 times your grubstake. Putting on a trade pulls every emotional cord we have. First, we will be either right or wrong. No one likes to be wrong (except experienced traders), and no one likes to lose money. Our brokers, our wife, our kids, our friends, and our enemies will all know how dumb we are. No one likes to look dumb, especially with their own money.

Because of this our decision-making process gets out of whack. Instead of approaching this like we do other decisions in our lives, we commit a terrible, yet very logical error:

We wait too long.

It goes something like this. We see a trade or investment setup. It looks pretty good, but since we operate from fear (good traders do not, by the way) we are afraid to take the trade. We are hesitant to jump aboard. After all, from the time we were kids we have been told, "Fools rush in where angels fear to tread." That axiom, for us, should be "Traders rush on where angels fear to trade."

Here's why. The public, acting out of fear, wants more approval of their idea. They have been told things like, "The majority is right," "Wait until the jury decides," and "Consensus rules." In the other parts of our lives this makes excellent sense, but not in trading.

Why that is true is very elementary. If we wait until the jury comes in, until all the votes have been cast, then that means by its very definition that the crowd has all bought. So I ask, who's left to drive prices higher so you can profit?

Right. No one.

You and I, dear fellow intrepid, need to buy, in advance of a push, from someone else. Then we need someone else to come into the game and push prices higher. If we wait until all the signs are clear, all the stoplights have turned green, soon there will be no more buyers.

The irony of the fear that traders have is that if you use stop-loss orders as I suggest, your worst possible loss is the same whether you buy before the crowd does or when they do. Am I making myself clear here?

With a stop-loss order in place your risk is the same, regardless of how good or bad the market looks. Your risk is your stop. My point is that you have a much better chance of not getting stopped out if you are buying when the public is selling than when they have been buying. Chart after chart, year after year, market after market have shown that to be a universal truth of speculation.

Now let's look at another example of the power of what I have just written as we examine the record of public buying in the actual marketplace of Treasury bonds from 2000 to 2004 (see Figure 5.9).

So, you ask, why do the buy signals work so well in bonds and not so hot in lumber? There are two answers. One I'll teach you right now. The other you may figure out or find the answer in a later chapter of this book. Note, though, that the sell signals, readings above the 75 percent dashed line, set up some pretty good sells in this market as well.

Let's look at one more market before wrapping up this chapter on how the public buys and sells commodities. What shall we look at? How about a market the public really likes? Yup, let's choose live hogs. And you ask, "Larry, how do you know the public likes this market?"

It's simply a matter of money. Hogs have one of the lowest margin deposits or requirements of all the commodities, so that's where you find a lot of small traders: where the admission cost is low (see Figure 5.10).

Wow! Look at how well the sells work here. Why, the very first one set up a gain of more than $4,000 on a $3,000 risk. Not bad, and this was not even the best of the sell opportunities set up by when the public became

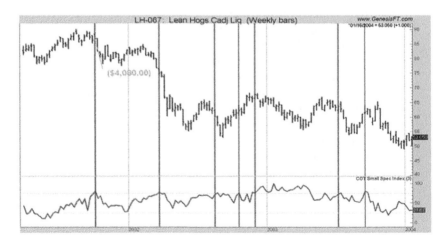

FIGURE 5.10 Lean Hogs Chart
Source: Genesis Financial Technologies, Inc. (www.GenesisFT.com).

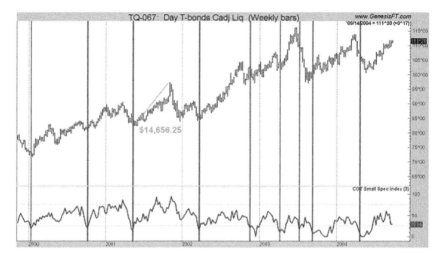

FIGURE 5.11

too bullish, falling for the flicking of the fly with a barbed hook skimming across their charts.

Also notice that there were only three times when the public got really bearish—mid-2001, the end of 2001, and the fall of 2003—and each time we got a pretty decent market rally. Ah, the public, ya gotta love 'em! They buy, we sell; they sell, we buy . . . what a simple rule!

Okay, we've looked at the commercials. We've studied the small traders. It's now time to look at the trading record of the group known as large traders, those who buy and sell in 100-lot sizes. That can be a chunk of change, like $2 million for 100 S&P contracts or $300,000 for 100 bonds. These guys have money—not as much as the commercials, but they sure have some weight to swing around—so let's find out how they trade . . . (see Figure 5.11).

CHAPTER 6

Large Traders . . . Not Quite As Good As You Think

The Big Boys were buying today.

Numerous times I've been told by brokers and fellow advisers that the big guys had come into the market on the buy or sell side as either an explanation of what happened or perhaps a hustle to get me on one side of the market. The truth of the matter is, as you will soon see, that the "Big Boys," the large traders from the "Commitments of Traders" (COT) report, do not have the stellar trading record you might expect.

There is a reason for that, which I will explain. First, though, let's take a look at their net long/short position in a variety of markets so we can get a sense of how they interact with price activity and see if their trading might help us.

I'll start with gold, for no particular reason other than it is widely followed and traded by the Big Boys all over the world. There are large positions—wagers if you will—plunked down every day in Hong Kong, Taiwan, London, Singapore, and Sydney on an assumption of the future direction of this market. Figure 6.1 shows the weekly price of gold and below it the net long/short position of the large traders.

This reading, when high, says they have been doing a lot more buying than selling. In fact, the further above the zero line, the more long positions they have. If the index is far below that line it means the large traders are on balance net short . . . that they have a lot more short positions on than longs.

It may help if you know just who the large traders really are. For the most part, these long and short positions reflect the action of the various commodity funds. Yes, some of the positions are from individual traders,

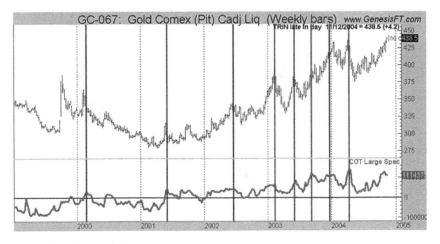

FIGURE 6.1 Gold Chart
Source: Genesis Financial Technologies, Inc. (www.GenesisFT.com).

but most of the action comes from guys and gals who run commodity funds, kind of like mutual funds. So think of them more as fund managers than individuals trading for themselves.

Let's now take a look at the gold market from 1999 through 2004 shown in Figure 6.1 and see how the large traders did during that time period in calling the highs and lows of this coveted metal. Keep in mind a high level means that they have been buying a great deal, and a low level means just the opposite—that they have been selling a great deal.

I have marked off the times when the large traders had their largest long positions and lookee, lookee . . . every time they got really long, by recent standards, the market declined!

Hmmm . . . not quite what you expected to see, is it?

Also notice that the times the net long/short position reading was low, meaning they were net short, coincide with some of the best buy points in that six-year window.

BETTER ON BONDS?

Let's turn our attention to how the large traders did in the bond market (Figure 6.2). You are looking at a weekly price chart and below it you see the net long/short large trader position. I have marked off the extremes of their long and short positions.

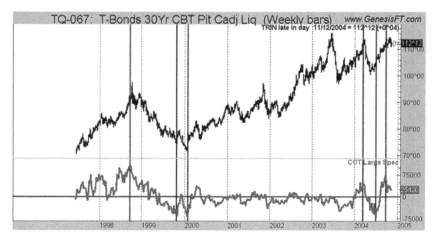

FIGURE 6.2 Treasury Bonds Chart
Source: Genesis Financial Technologies, Inc. (www.GenesisFT.com).

What we see here is pretty amazing, that at the very best sell points the large traders had on their largest, most bullish positions. And check out the lows. At the extreme lows the large traders had on their largest short positions. They were looking for lower prices right at the low. They could not have been more incorrect if they had tried!

BONDS AND GOLD ARE SURE NOT COWS

Treasury bonds are a creation of mankind, and the price of gold is often a reflection of interest rates. Both may move more due to politics, war scare, and inflation than will an agricultural commodity like cattle. So next I'd like to share with you a weekly cattle chart versus the large traders net position (see Figure 6.3).

I have again marked off the times that the large traders were the most bullish, the times they had an excessive number of long contracts versus short contracts. The ensuing market declines are a thing of beauty to a short seller. Time after time, we see that the large traders are the most bullish at a market high, the most bearish—with real money I might add—at market lows. It does not matter what market they work. They seem to always be heavy buyers of market highs and sellers of market lows.

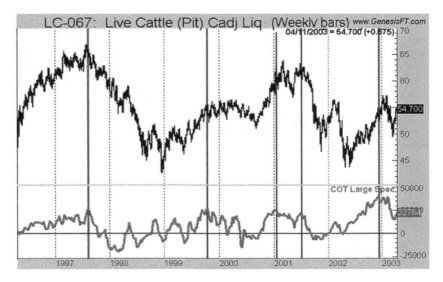

FIGURE 6.3   Live Cattle Chart
Source: Genesis Financial Technologies, Inc. (www.GenesisFT.com).

HOW DO THEY STAY LARGE TRADERS?

Indeed, one can only ask how this group became large traders and how they can continue in the game with such an apparently poor track record.

You need to understand the dynamics of the marketplace to understand what is going on here. Remember how I told you that the large traders are, for the most part, commodity fund managers? That's the key to getting the real picture of what you have just seen. These fund managers, for the most part, trade in a particular style and it is that style, their way of doing business, that gives what appears to be very poor performance. I say that because the commodity fund managers are, for the most part, long-term trend followers.

Trend followers of this nature don't just buy one time and wait for the fireworks. Additionally, the stronger the trend becomes the more positions trend followers will have in a market. Here's a simple example. Corn begins a long-lasting bull move going from $2.30 per bushel to $3.40, a potential gain of $6,000 on an investment of less than $1,000.

As the move begins, some of the smarter or more short-term trend-oriented funds begin to see the up move in price, and thus buy corn. Their entry price is the highest high of the last 20 days. Let's say they purchase 1,000 contracts as a group. They are correct, as corn continues rallying. Since the trend is up they will not sell (their sell or exit comes from a change in trend). They are in for the ride. About this time another group of managers who have a little slower or longer-term trend-following method become buyers and establish their longs. Their computers have flashed a buy signal at the highest high of the last 40 days. So they step in and buy 1,000 contracts.

Corn continues rallying, now hitting the highest high of the last 26 weeks, a place I know lots of funds will become buyers. So another group takes down another 1,000 contracts. Most funds are now long as there has not been a pullback that would shake any of them out of their positions.

Next comes the highest high of the last 52 weeks and a bunch of funds step up to the plate at this point. Again 1,000 more contracts are entered in the long side by the super-long-term trend followers. All the fund managers combined now have a total of 4,000 contracts to the long side.

What happens next is not pretty. The market starts to come down, taking out the lowest low of the last 20 days, where the first 1,000 lots are liquidated at a profit. Prices rally back to a new 20-day high. So the first group gets back in, and again there are 4,000 longs and perhaps another 1,000 or more based on this last trend move.

By the time all this has happened corn has climbed to the $3.40 per bushel area and on balance all the funds have an average cost of $2.80 a bushel. The bull reigns supreme as corn climbs a little and then begins to collapse.

Accountants know what is first in, first out (FIFO) and last in, first out (LIFO) when it comes to sales and inventories. When it comes to the marketplace and trend following, it's strictly a FIFO business. The FIFO corn guys who bought really early in the up move will use a similar trend exit point. So once the price falls below a 30-day low, lots of them leave the party, before funds who take a longer-term view of trend analysis. They can make money at this when the advance has taken the price up so much that the 30-day low leaves plenty of profits for them. The same goes for the next entry-level guys, who get out with a profit. The fellows who bought at a 52-week high will get out at a 52-week low, so they stay long through the decline. For the sake of discussion a new 52-week low is not hit, so they are still net long.

See what happened? The stronger the trend was, the more buyers it attracted. So at the end of a trend, there will be numerous funds and large traders long, who still make a profit as their exit point is above their entry point.

The large speculator is typically a large floor trader, a managed futures account, or a small hedge fund. In general, these types of traders are technically oriented trend followers. Since the large speculators category are consistent trend followers and usually overdo it at extremes, we want to "fade" the large speculators, as they are usually wrong.

If you want to get a good long-term view of commodities, it is best to do so from the hedgers' or commercials' point of view. Why is this? The hedgers are the most important. They have access to the cash markets, which gives them a large advantage. They are buying and selling in cash markets every day and thus have a better sense of actual market prices. Hedgers have superior information. They operate from the "smart money" point of view.

When the net position of the large speculators is at an extreme, expect the market to move in the opposite direction of the net position of the large speculators. For instance, if the large speculators are net long—and the net position is at an extreme and prices have been moving up—expect the price of the commodity to correct down.

The large traders can and do make money when they catch a trend move, but such strong trends are rare. I estimate markets are in strong trend moves only about one-third of the time, and even then at some point the commercials come and take control. There is a greater chance that the commercials will be correct. The times we have to be careful are when there are very strong, tight uptrends or downtrends.

UNDERSTANDING THE COT REPORT

We can make more order out of this when we recall that the COT report lists the number of longs and shorts—the total position. It does not tell us when traders got in, only the number of contracts they are long and short. Knowing that the more a market rallies the more longs will be added, it is only logical that close to the end of an uptrend the trend followers (translate that to fund managers) will have on their most bullish position. What's critically important is to realize that not all the longs were put on right then at the end of the trend; the positions were added over the trend move and just naturally will be greater the longer a trend lasts.

HOW THE FUNDS TRADE—X MARKS THE SPOT

Based on what you have learned, if my assumption is correct, we should pretty well be able to figure out what makes the funds jump aboard a trend. All we need to do is look to see if their net position increases when a new X week high is made or the net position decreases at an X week low. In other words, if we see the funds taking action consistently at the X week point, we know that is their "sweet spot" of trend identification.

Where is X? Let's take a look. On the chart of cotton (Figure 6.4), I

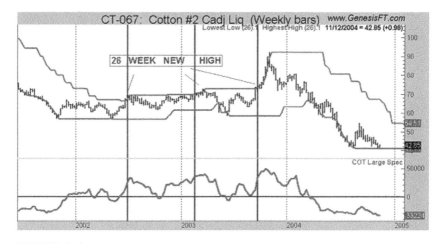

FIGURE 6.4 Cotton Chart
Source: Genesis Financial Technologies, Inc. (www.GenesisFT.com).

have placed a line showing the highest high and low of the last 26 weeks. Notice how when the price rallies to that level the funds dramatically increase their buying, putting them net long a large amount (as I have marked off with the vertical lines).

The other side of this coin is equally revealing. When prices drop to the 26-week low channel line, the net position line dips a great deal, telling us the funds have now exited their longs and have increased their short position. This is particularly evident at the end of the first quarter of 2004 when prices touched the 26-week low line and this was followed by the very low level in the large traders net position. The data was clear: the funds used this as a time to sell.

This is not unique to cotton; it is true of all markets the funds dabble in. Let's turn our attention to the Canadian dollar (Figure 6.5), a market that is totally different from cotton except for one thing: the funds' net long position increases dramatically as a new 26-week high is made and decreases in the middle of 2004 when a new 26-week low is touched.

From our study of the actual buying and selling of this group, I think it is fair to say they are heavily reliant on channels, moving averages, and such that use the 26-week time period as their entry point.

To give more insight into this idea I'm next showing a chart of hogs, another market disparate from what we have seen before. On this chart (Figure 6.6) the vertical lines mark each time hogs closed above or below the 26-week channel, so that you can then see the large trader position for that week. There is high correlation between new 26-week highs and lows and what the managers of money do. New 26-week highs are accompanied by

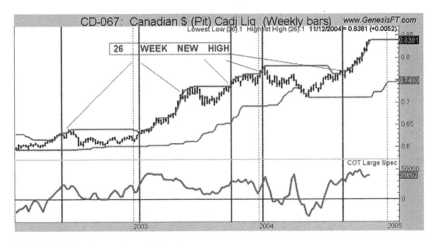

FIGURE 6.5   Canadian Dollar Chart
Source: Genesis Financial Technologies, Inc. (www.GenesisFT.com).

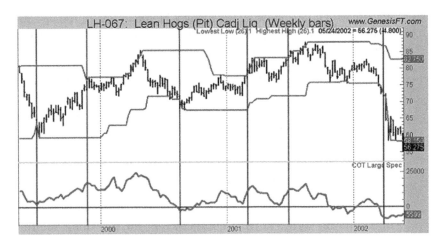

FIGURE 6.6   Lean Hogs Chart
Source: Genesis Financial Technologies, Inc. (www.GenesisFT.com).

large increases in the net long position, while new 26-week lows habitually see a decline in the net long position, something that can happen only when they are sellers and/or short sellers.

THE INDEX APPROACH TO LOOKING AT THE LARGE TRADERS

We can use the same math to look at the large traders as we did when we developed the COT index for the commercials or small traders. It's the exact same formula. The only difference is that when the large traders index is above 80 we want to look for sells, and when it is below 20 we want to look for buys. In essence we want to do the opposite of what the large traders do. A few charts should illustrate the wisdom of this approach.

Let's begin with soybeans, perhaps the most important "grain" grown in the world due to its multi-usage in everything from soap to ice cream, tofu to soybean pseudo milk products (see Figure 6.7).

In the six years shown here, there can be no doubt that the best buy times came when the large trader index was below 20, the best sells when above 80. It is not a precise "sell today" index, but rather an excellent setup tool, telling us to get ready for the next major trend move in the market.

The next chart to look at is coffee (Figure 6.8). Here's a market that was in a trading range for several years. It's noteworthy to see that at

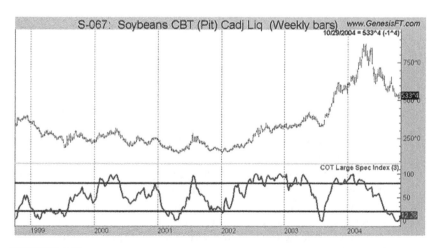

FIGURE 6.7 Soybeans Chart
Source: Genesis Financial Technologies, Inc. (www.GenesisFT.com).

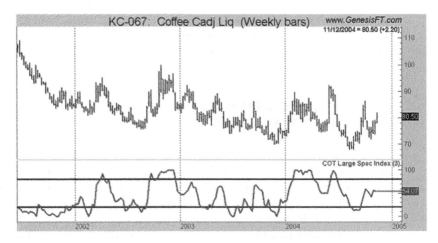

FIGURE 6.8 Coffee Chart
Source: Genesis Financial Technologies, Inc. (www.GenesisFT.com).

every one of the highs the large traders, the trend-following funds, went long. We know this because the large trader index is above 80 at these points, time after time. The reverse is equally true; at the lows the index was under 20, telling us large traders were heavy sellers.

I often post current examples on Larry Live at my website: www.ireallytrade.com. There you will continue to see the importance of facing the large traders.

Later on I will tie all three of these indexes together so you can see how the commercials, large traders, and small traders stack up against one another. But for now, I hope you have seen the light and gotten the message: that we want to do the opposite of the large traders when they are at an extreme.

It is at their extremes that we can take action. When all the fund managers' trend systems are in, the market is about to top. Here's why.

When the funds have committed all they have to one side or another, there is no one left to move the market any further in that direction.

When a car is out of gas it can't go any further. When all the fund buying power is used up it's very hard for a market rally to continue. The funds can be right, but when they gang up they are most apt to be wrong, something we can take advantage of as private speculators.

There's one lesson here for sure. The next time someone tells you that the Big Boys have been big buyers, look to go short!

CHAPTER 7

The Facts
on Volume

What's the use of happiness? It can't buy you money.

The net effect of commercials, large traders, and small traders can be expressed in two ways. The first is what traders refer to as volume: how many contracts of a commodity traded for a day, week, month, or whatever time period one is studying. Since price cannot move without buying and selling volume, analysts have spent a great deal of time trying to learn how it fits into the equation. (The second way is open interest, discussed in the next chapter.)

It's very hard to say any one technical indicator is the most misunderstood, as they are all deceitful, often merely placebos and rarely of great value on their own. I would, however, rate volume right up there at the top of the list of old wives' tales of technical analysis.

How many times have I read or been told that advancing price on advancing volume is bullish, as is declining price on declining volume? Hundreds is my estimate. Just as often, I have read the opposite to be equally true; a rally in price on declining volume is bearish, and a decline in price on increasing volume even more so. Book after book on stocks and commodities have made these assertions, to the point that they are widely accepted as true.

It's not entirely clear why these assertions have been put forth. They sound logical, I guess, and the comments have been passed from one generation of trader to the next, by word of mouth, books, and now the web pages.

I'm not here to make a case one way or the other about this relationship. I'm here to determine the truth, what works, and here is what I have found.

The eight equity curves that follow show the full history of the S&P 500 from 1990 to 2004, using an entry of buying on the open and exiting on the first profitable close or using a $3,500 stop. None of the following patterns are tradable as such, but each pattern will help us better understand the supposed impact of price and volume. The equity curves show the net profits for trading the patterns. The ideal equity curve, of course, would start at zero and smoothly and rapidly increase over time.

The first clip (Figure 7.1) shows what happens if we buy when a five-day moving average of price is greater than the prior day and at the same time the five-day moving average of volume is greater than the prior day. *Both price and volume are in uptrends.*

The equity chart of such a trading strategy does not appear to offer much hope, at least for the short-term trader. In fact, the concept has been

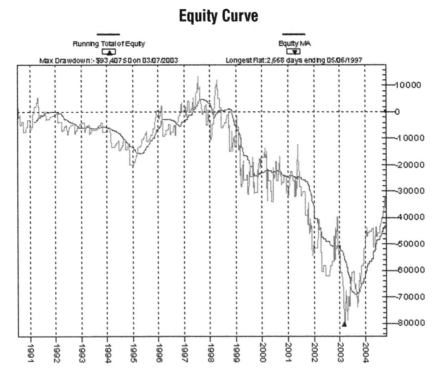

FIGURE 7.1 S&P 500—Price Up, Volume Up

a net loser over the past 15 years. The data suggests to me that a condition of advancing prices on advancing volume is not bullish.

THE OTHER SIDE OF THE COIN

Let's next look at the equity line of buying when the five-day moving average of price is greater than the prior day while the five-day moving average of volume is less than the prior day (see Figure 7.2). Here we have *advancing price on declining volume*, something the so-called experts of the business tell us is bearish.

While not wildly bullish, the equity line from this strategy is certainly better than the price/volume pattern that is generally put forth as being bullish. Interesting, isn't it!

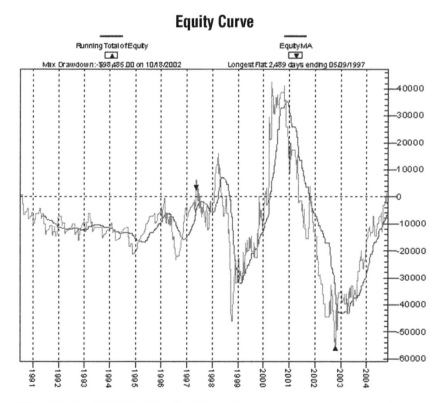

FIGURE 7.2 S&P 500—Price Up, Volume Down

ONE DAY MATTERS?

Perhaps it is wrong to be looking at the five-day direction of price and volume, so let's go to the start and look at just one day's activity. Our first look will be to see if *both price and volume are down* for the day and buy on the next opening. This, the technicians say, is the most bullish price-to-volume relationship on a down close. Figure 7.3 shows what that equity line looks like.

The other side of this coin is a down close day while volume increases or expands from the prior day (see Figure 7.4). *Price down, volume up,* a relationship the chartists tell us is bearish. I'll let you judge for yourself how bearish this is. It does not appear bearish to me, and in fact it looks more tradable and "trend-able" than the other way around . . . but then, I'm old, my eyes don't work so well anymore, and I'm a bit biased on this volume stuff.

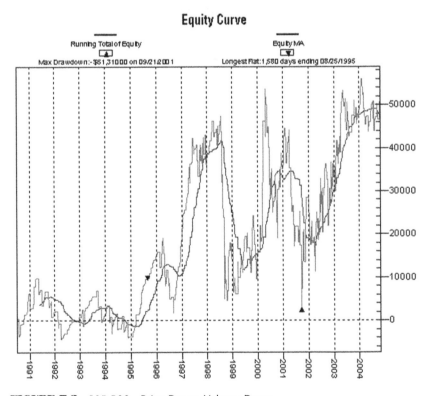

FIGURE 7.3 S&P 500—Price Down, Volume Down

Equity Curve

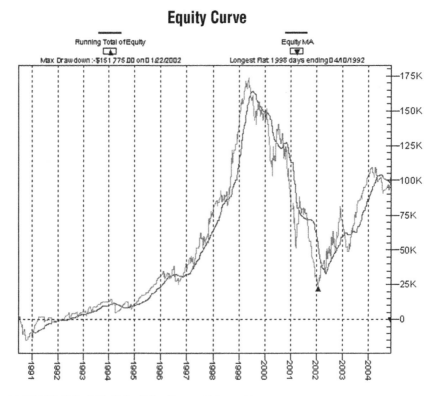

Running Total of Equity   Equity MA

Max Drawdown :-$151 775.00 on 0 1/22/2002 Longest Flat 1 998 days ending 0 4/10/1992

FIGURE 7.4 S&P 500—Price Down, Volume Up

THERE IS ANOTHER WAY TO LOOK AT THIS RELATIONSHIP

The next step was to take a much longer view of price and volume. Figure 7.5 shows the results of the same entry, but only when a 50-day moving average of price is down and over the past eight days both the moving averages of price and volume are higher—a down market scenario with a *rally that has seen a pickup in volume.*

ANOTHER LOOK AT THAT TWO-SIDED COIN

The next chart of this series is the same as Figure 7.5 in that it shows a 50-day downtrend in price with a shorter-term 8-day uptrend in price, but

Equity Curve

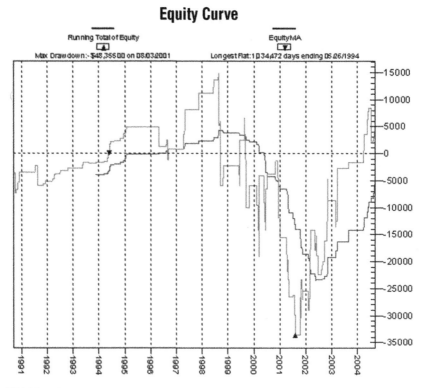

Running Total of Equity　　　　　　　　　　　EquityMA

Max Drawdown:-$48,355.00 on 08.03.2001　　　Longest Flat:1,034,472 days ending 05.26/1994

FIGURE 7.5 S&P 500—Long-Term Price Down, Short-Term Price and Volume Up

this time the 8-day moving average of volume is lower than the prior day. (See Figure 7.6.) In essence, what we have is *longer-term downtrend and short-term uptrend with declining volume.* This does not appear as good a buy setup as the prior example, and may support the idea of price up, volume down as being bearish to a slight extent . . . a suggestion, a hint, but certainly not an overpowering be-all and end-all secret to market success.

ONE LAST LOOK

If I've lost everyone by now, take heart: the next charts are perhaps the most meaningful. The first one (Figure 7.7) looks at the same price lower than 50 days ago but also requires the 8-day moving average of price to be

Equity Curve

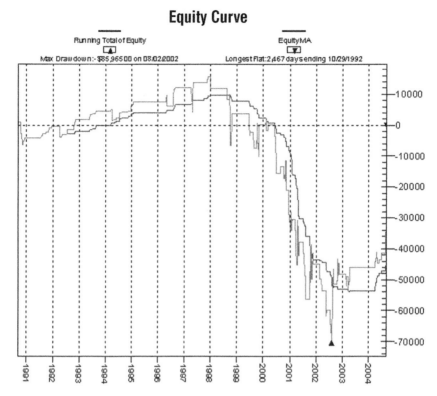

Max Drawdown:-$85,965.00 on 08/02/2002   Longest Flat:2,467 days ending 10/29/1992

FIGURE 7.6 S&P 500—Long-Term Price Down, Short-Term Price Up, Short-Term Volume Down

down while *the 8-day moving average of volume has been up.* The books will tell us that this is bearish and lower prices should ensue or at least not set up for market rallies. That's because price has declined on heavier volume, a pattern 99.9 percent of investment authors see as bearish. The S&P 500 apparently did not read the books, as a quick study of the equity curve from trading this relationship shows.

Our last clip, Figure 7.8, is the same setup as Figure 7.7 but the *8-day moving average of volume has been down.*

The most money has been made by what the trading and investing books say is the most bearish—a decline in price on an increase in volume—and appears, again, to be less erratic and thus more tradable than the other way around.

Equity Curve

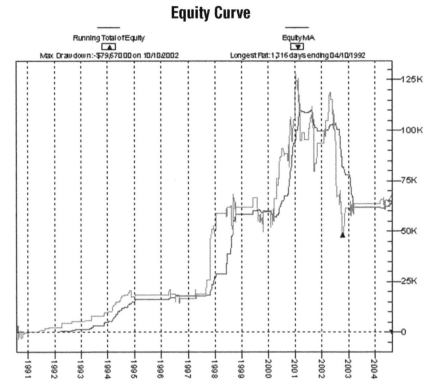

FIGURE 7.7 S&P 500—Long-Term and Short-Term Price Down, Short-Term Volume Up

A LONGER-TERM VIEW OF VOLUME

Enough with the S&P 500; let's look at a globally followed market, the British pound. Figure 7.9 reflects a simple strategy of exiting 20 days after a volume/price pattern. To test these patterns no stop was used, so the worst possible thing could happen in the trade: it could go straight down forever. The price-to-volume setup was to look at the direction of the moving average of price and compare that to the moving average direction of volume. In all instances the moving averages of price and volume were the same; for example, a 60-day moving average of price was compared to a 60-day moving average of volume.

Equity Curve

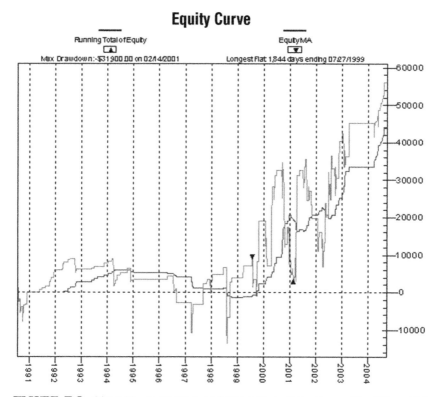

FIGURE 7.8 S&P 500—Long-Term and Short-Term Price Down, Short-Term Volume Down

In the first clip (Figure 7.9) we see the results of the trend of both price and volume being up; the moving average of each was greater than two days ago. *Price up, volume up,* the supposed bullish relationship, made some money here (showing a gain of $20,123 on 127 trades for an average gain of $157). The equity chart gives us a view of how easy or hard the winnings were to come by.

A market rally on lower volume is supposed to be bearish, as it suggests the rally cannot gain any more steam. The absence of increasing volume is supposed to mean the market is moving into weak hands, or large players have lost interest in the rally. Is that right or wrong? When I tested as before but with price in an uptrend and volume in a downtrend, I found 133 trades made $9,028 with an average gain of $68 (see

Equity Curve

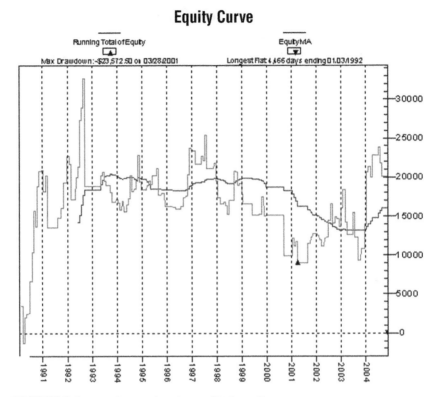

FIGURE 7.9 British Pound—Price and Volume Up

Figure 7.10). A cursory look at the all-telling equity line shows there is merit to this idea.

I next tested what happened when both price and volume were in downtrends to see what bearing this relationship had on the future performance of the pound. The test showed 99 trades making $6,983 with an average profit per trade of $71. Nothing to trade for, in any way whatsoever (see Figure 7.11), because as you can see from the equity chart, it was a rocky road for anyone using this price and volume relationship for buying. It should be noted this pattern was better than price down volume up (discussed next).

The final test of this series is what the chartist writers and techni-

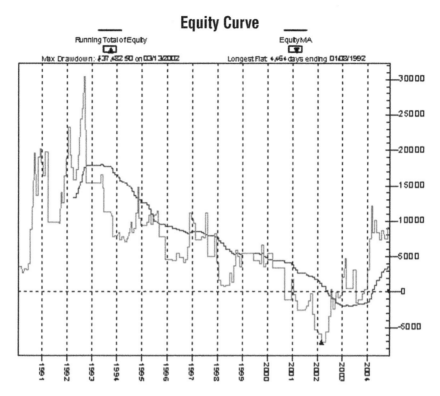

FIGURE 7.10 British Pound—Price Up, Volume Down

cians say is the most bearish: price down and volume up. Their comments have bounced off the halls and walls of Wall Street for more than 150 years, claiming that this is an increase in selling pressure and a sign of lower prices yet to come. My test did not confirm that view. I found 102 trades making $42,673 with an average profit per trade of $487 . . . 61 percent winners and wins 1.22 times more than losing trades (see Figure 7.12).

This is the same bullishness we found in the S&P 500 studies on the open to close—that a situation of lower prices on increasing volume is *bullish*, not bearish! This pattern made more than twice as much as what is supposed to be bullish, price and volume up. More telling is

Equity Curve

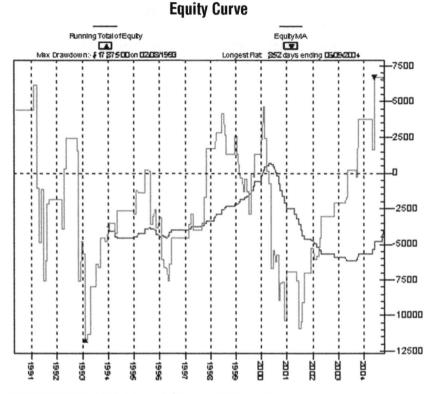

FIGURE 7.11 British Pound—Price and Volume Down

the ease of the equity line shown here. While the other equity lines danced all over the place, here we see a smooth and consistent uptrend. The message seems pretty clear to me: price down and volume up is bullish.

CONFESSION TIME

It seems that the volume/price relationships that matter and that are the most correct as a rule of thumb are:

- Price up, volume down is bearish.
- Price down, volume up is bullish.

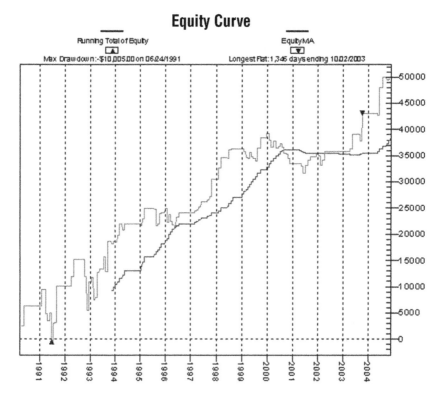

FIGURE 7.12   British Pound—Price Down, Volume Up

However, there is more—much more—than meets the eye here. You see, when I run this same test on other markets I get *different results*. A case in point is the bond market. There the most bullish relationship is price up and volume down! This was the worst for most markets I studied but the best for bonds. The equity chart shown in Figure 7.13 looks like a pretty good trading strategy.

This system was 63 percent correct, making more than $529 a trade with a small $12,000 drawdown. Compare that with price down and volume up, which made $12,543, or price and volume both up, which made $16,365, or price down and volume down, which cleared $266 on 92 trades!

How can this be? If price change is caused by volume, how come there is nothing consistent about the traditional price/volume relationships?

Equity Curve

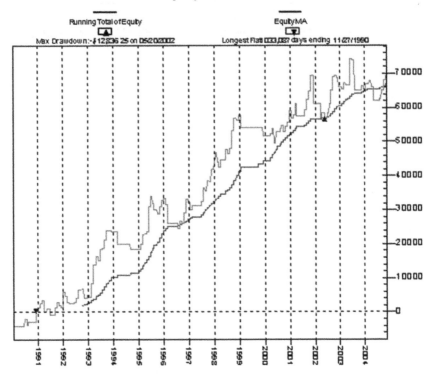

FIGURE 7.13 Bonds—Price Up, Volume Down (Bullish)

SUMMATION

This chapter has presented lots of charts to look at and ponder their meaning—if any. The question of whether there is—or is not—anything of value in the price/volume relationship needs more work. To which I say, "Stay tuned"—we are not through with this subject.

CHAPTER 8

The Breakthrough

Getting Inside Volume and Open Interest

I saw a man with a wooden leg and a real foot.

While most people understand that stocks move due to volume, many stock players are not familiar with one of the major differences between stocks and commodities. This difference is open interest (OI). Unlike stocks, this is a zero-sum game. For every dollar won, a dollar is lost. There is always a total of all the short positions, called short open interest. On the other side of the coin there is long open interest, the total of all the positions initiated on the long side. Total open interest is the net of these two numbers and has been suggested by numerous authors as a key tool to understanding market moves.

The difference between volume and OI should be noted. We may have a day that trades, for example, 550,000 contracts. That's the total of buying and selling contracts for the day. Many of these buys and sells may have been closed out during the day by day traders or by short-term traders exiting a trade from a prior day. Open interest, in contrast, is the net number of contracts at the end of the day.

Let me explain. In the stock market a company issues a certain number of shares (float), and that's it—there are no more shares to trade. In commodities there is no finite number of contracts or float. It is open ended. As long as a new buyer comes in and there is a new seller, OI will increase. At times there may be more volume (i.e., contracts traded) than total OI.

Open interest applies primarily to the futures market. Open interest, or the total number of open contracts on a security, is often used to confirm trends and trend reversals for futures and options contracts. It is important to understand that a contract has both a buyer and a seller, so the two players combine to make one contract. The OI position that is reported each day represents the increase or decrease in the number of contracts for that day, and it is shown as a positive or negative number. An increase in OI along with an increase in price is said to confirm an upward trend. Similarly, an increase in OI along with a decrease in price confirms a downward trend. An increase or decrease in prices while OI remains flat or declining may indicate a possible trend reversal . . . or so the experts say.

When I think of OI I think of a swimming pool on a hot summer day. It may be that 10,000 people visit the pool for some exercise or cooling (that's total volume). Yet when it's closing time, there are only 1,000 visitors left at the pool (that's OI). In the markets, though, it is a rare event when there is more volume than OI. If and when that takes place it means that the market has become rampant with day traders and short-term speculation.

A KEY POINT ON OPEN INTEREST

Perhaps a better way to think of OI is that it is exactly what it says it is—interest in a market. The more contracts open, the larger the interest in the market has become. Thus an increase in OI is saying that someone is very excited about what the market is doing—going up or down. I think of OI as participation or interest in a market, and know that when OI is increasing someone (I'll get to that in the next chapter) thinks the current trend is valid. They are climbing on board that price trend.

A large OI tells us, for the most part, that the crowd or masses are in the marketplace, and they are usually found to be wrong. When OI is very low, the public has no interest in the market—it's a pure commercial market. Usually this is where major up moves begin, when the public has no appetite to be buyers. Never take another man's bet. He wouldn't offer it to you if he wasn't thinking that he knew something you didn't.

Many analysts have looked at the relationship of OI to price movements and have stepped forward with pretty hard rules of how to use OI. These rules (the conventional wisdom) are:

- Open interest up, price up is bullish.
- Open interest up, price down is bearish.
- Open interest down, price up is bearish.
- Open interest down, price down is bullish.

Remember, this is conventional wisdom. I do not say it is correct!

Book after book has regurgitated this view of price trend and OI for the past 50 years, and while at times, like any good placebo, it is correct, it can also be equally incorrect. A placebo works about 33 percent of the time, and I'd say that is just about the rate of effectiveness of the standard thinking on OI. About one-third of the time the conventional wisdom works, but the problem is we are trading three-thirds of the time!

Typical comments on OI are:

In an uptrending market, if the longs are increasing their positions and the losers (the shorts—we know they are losers as prices are rallying) are being replaced, open interest will be increasing.

When open interest declines as prices increase, what are the longs doing? They are selling out their long positions, taking profits.

An ideal bear market is seen with prices moving lower on increasing open interest.

Let's look at some examples of OI and price to see what we can learn about these basic rules.

In the case of Figure 8.1, the soybeans chart, we can see important market tops that were associated with increases in price and OI, a supposedly bullish pattern that did not turn out that way in real life. Learning

FIGURE 8.1 Soybeans Chart
Source: Genesis Financial Technologies, Inc. (www.GenesisFT.com).

often consists of learning what not to learn. That's so often the case in this business. Here it is in black and white: soybeans topped out on an increasing OI. That's not what the books teach about the markets, but then, books don't trade.

In Figure 8.2, the April 2001 low in soybeans developed on what is supposed to be bearish—a decline in price while there is a large increase in OI. Typical tea-leaf readers of OI would say a downtrend with increasing open interest means shorts are adding to their positions while longs (the losers in this case) are still increasing their longs. So the shorts are in control, and a further decline is to be expected. How can it be that OI picks up dramatically just before the market bottoms—that while the price is falling there is a pickup of interest in this market? That's not the model that we are told markets follow.

Two months later, though, soybeans do what they are supposed to: price declines, as does OI, telling us new shorts are not being added. Hence an up move can be expected, and that's just what happens. It's the placebo effect at work. There's nothing harder to unlearn than what seems to be the truth when it is only random luck. This is the typical bullish pattern that has been passed down from one generation of market watchers to the next. As you can see, at times it does work.

Randomness, the great muse of all market players, is one tough cookie to deal with. I have been fooled by this flirtatious siren more times than I care to admit. We see two things together, then notice an apparent cause or effect from that coupling. The truth is that the outcome was

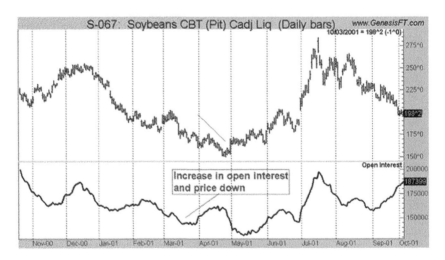

FIGURE 8.2 Soybeans Daily Chart
Source: Genesis Financial Technologies, Inc. (www.GenesisFT.com).

caused by some third party hiding behind a tree, or by no explainable cause at all.

So, these authors and advisers can find examples to validate their beliefs. But just as often, if not more so, we can find the opposite to be equally true. All this is well and good and makes for interesting discussion. Yet the lack of consistency is something I cannot put up with as one who ekes out a living trading, not writing for fun and pleasure. I know I'm not going to be right all the time, but dang it all, I'd like to be right more than 30 percent of the time! And I'd like to see under scrutiny some consistency. Why the discrepancy? Simple, one key point is sadly missing in standard OI analysis.

OPEN INTEREST AS A TIMING OR ENTRY TOOL

As you recall, earlier I touched on the point that OI gives us a good idea of how many swimmers are in the pool. In this business of speculating, when everyone is in the pool the market is closer to a turning point, usually down. By the same token, when no one is in the pool, it's a great time to get in and usually markets rally. There is a natural reason for this. Price action (trend) attracts buyers and short sellers. Hence there is *almost always* an increase of players (OI) on rallies. When a market has become dull (no price moves), investors shy away. But, as you will soon see, that is usually the wrong thing to do. More market bottoms and excellent buy points have been formed when OI is low than at any other time. Equally true is this statement: more market highs have been made when OI is higher than at any other time.

Low OI means that the public and funds have lost interest in this particular market. Their attention and money have been diverted elsewhere. Since I live and die by the notion the public is wrong (I know this from personal experience; they voted for some other guy to be their United States Senator from Montana. See how wrong they can be!), the fact that the public is not interested in a market means I should be. Of course this is just a concept, a concept though that I can prove to you, thanks to the record of OI.

MY OPEN INTEREST INDICATOR

Realizing this means we can begin to put OI into perspective and use it to help us select markets ready to rally or decline. I'll start this lesson with soybeans, a popular trading market. Noting the indicator in Figure 8.3, the price action is simply a 12-month stochastic of OI. What we are looking at

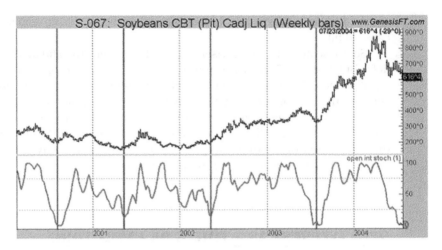

FIGURE 8.3 Soybeans Weekly Chart
Source: Genesis Financial Technologies, Inc. (www.GenesisFT.com).

here is not price, not the commercials, not the public, and not the large traders. Simply put, we are looking at the ebb and tide of total speculative interest in soybeans. What is apparent is that when there is little speculative interest, the market is a better buy than the other way around.

This is not an anomaly to soybeans. It is a truism of all markets. As an example I'll next proffer up gold (see Figure 8.4). While a low OI indication

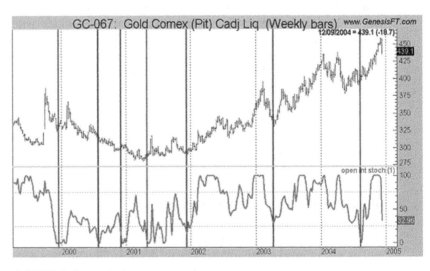

FIGURE 8.4 Gold Chart
Source: Genesis Financial Technologies, Inc. (www.GenesisFT.com).

does not mark every bottom, every good buy point is concurrent with a low OI reading. Get that? While at times OI does not call the exact low (I wish it was that easy), we can still pretty much rest assured that almost all lows will come hand in glove with this important market indication. This is like the comment that all cognac is brandy, but not all brandy is cognac. In short, we can narrow down times to look for major plays in the market . . . and that's a huge advantage.

Let's look at a few more markets to drive home this point, and discuss what markets this does not work in—notably stock index futures. The financial markets have a much different OI pattern as there is no physical crop of stocks or British pounds to bring to the marketplace, so the interest in the market is synthetic and involves a great deal of arbitrage between markets. This accounts for spikes in OI close to delivery, with a large buildup of OI, then a sharp drop-off as the new contract begins trading. Nonetheless, as Figure 8.5, a chart of the pound, shows, the idea of a low OI reading has great merit.

Even such thin and mundane markets as lumber respond to this phenomenon of lack of interest as a warning to the speculator to get interested. (See Figure 8.6.) While far from perfect (nothing is perfect in this business), the notion of low OI is one that sets up many excellent buying points, while a high OI reading in this index usually precedes market tops.

The S&P 500 and Dow Jones Industrial Average present us with a

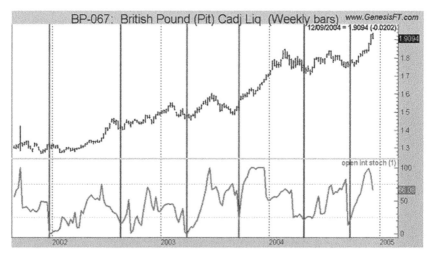

FIGURE 8.5 British Pound Chart
Source: Genesis Financial Technologies, Inc. (www.GenesisFT.com).

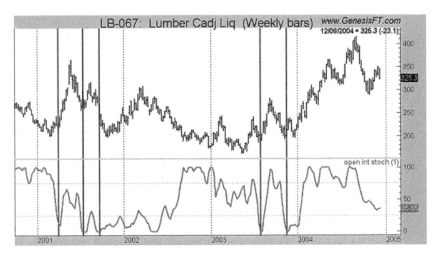

FIGURE 8.6 Lumber Chart
Source: Genesis Financial Technologies, Inc. (www.GenesisFT.com).

different set of problems due to the liquidation of the contracts four times per year at expiration. Figure 8.7 shows a recent example of that so you can see for yourself, and learn not to rely on OI by itself for these contracts.

We will have to attack the stock market from a different direction. What should be apparent here, however, is that most of the major sell-offs

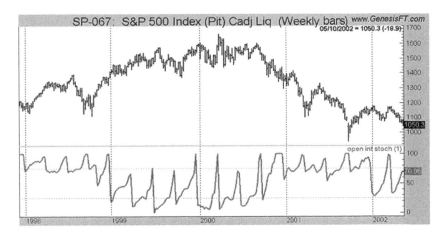

FIGURE 8.7 S&P 500 Index Chart
Source: Genesis Financial Technologies, Inc. (www.GenesisFT.com).

began with a high OI level, a point to keep in mind. In many ways this is like contrary opinion: the notion that the crowd can never be right, and that when the majority is of one mind they are most apt to be wrong. While that idea gives great solace to guys like John Kerry or Richard Nixon, it gives even more comfort to a trader to be able to know, based on actual numbers, what the crowd is doing so that we do not follow them over the cliff leading to speculative ruins.

SELLS IN SILVER

Let's look at a long-term chart of silver and the OI indicator. It takes only a glance at Figure 8.8 to see that the major highs in this market came at a time when OI was high.

This is not a recent phenomenon of silver and OI. As you can see from Figure 8.9, the next weekly chart going back to 1993 (so we have covered the last 12 years), the same pattern was alive and well back then as it is now. High OI levels are associated with market peaks and low levels with market bottoms.

Finally, to drive the point home Figure 8.10 shows silver all the way back to 1985, where again we see the same operative rule. Etch this one into your skull. Write it in on your chart book. High levels of OI, as measured by a one-year stochastic indicator, are bearish and are usually seen shortly before a significant top.

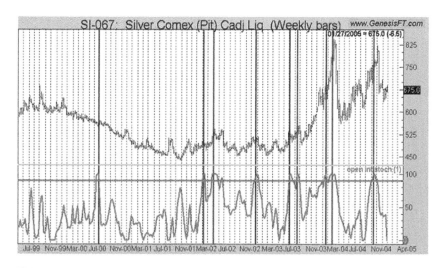

FIGURE 8.8 Silver Chart
Source: Genesis Financial Technologies, Inc. (www.GenesisFT.com).

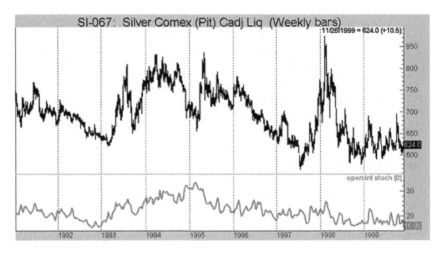

FIGURE 8.9   Silver Weekly Chart
Source: Genesis Financial Technologies, Inc. (www.GenesisFT.com).

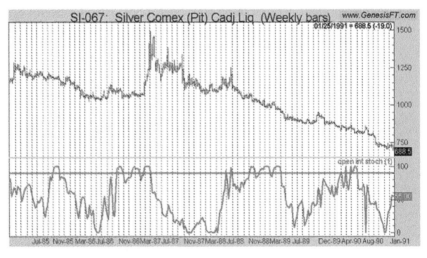

FIGURE 8.10   Silver Weekly Chart
Source: Genesis Financial Technologies, Inc. (www.GenesisFT.com).

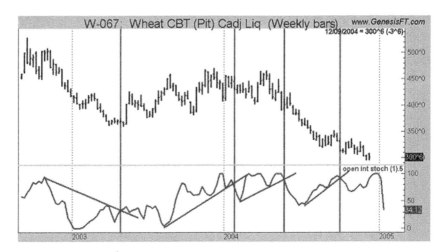

FIGURE 8.11 Wheat Chart
Source: Genesis Financial Technologies, Inc. (www.GenesisFT.com).

BUYING AND SELLING

If you look at all of the examples one more time, you will notice that when the very low OI readings began to turn up, so did the trend of the market in most instances—the point being that we can use the change or momentum of OI to tell us when to get into a market position.

Let's look at a simple way of using this concept. Figure 8.11 is a chart of wheat. It shows the 12-month stochastic. All that I have added are simple trend lines on the OI indicator to suggest when we should look for our entry. The operating rule here is that when the indicator is high, look for trend breaks to the downside for sells. When it is low, take trend breaks to the upside as potential buy entries. What I like about this is that we are not using price to forecast price. A cannot predict A. We are using the interest of all the players in the market to suggest our forays into trying to guess the future.

The lesson is that OI can be very helpful to us. Think of it as the masses, the crowd. Markets by their very nature cannot have everyone buying the lows and selling the highs. However, the opposite, buying the highs and selling the lows, is true. So look for times when there is no OI if you want to find a market that is going to get really interesting.

CHAPTER 9

Opening Up on Open Interest

The question is not if open interest (OI) is increasing or decreasing, but who is causing the change—weak hands like the public or strong hands like the commercials?

That's the question that needs to be answered. So what if prices are rallying in a nice uptrend. The telling issue is whether a concomitant increase in OI is being caused by the public adding long positions while the commercials are decreasing their longs or the commercials adding longs while the public is doing the selling. It's not so much OI that controls the market as it is who (which side or team) is controlling OI.

With that in mind, let's go back to the first chart presented in the preceding chapter, where we saw that an increase in OI actually led to market tops, something that is not supposed to happen. This time, though (see Figure 9.1), I have shown not only OI but also the commercials' net long/short position, the dotted line. This line goes up when they are adding longs or closing out shorts and down when they are selling shorts or exiting longs. Now we have the ability to look inside OI to see what the major players in the game, the commercials, are doing and how that relates to OI.

What we see is that the OI increase in October 2003 was not caused by the commercials. They were leaving or selling. So who caused the increase? There are only two other parties, large or small traders. They are the ones that created the increase in OI, adding to long positions at the wrong time—just as a market high was forming!

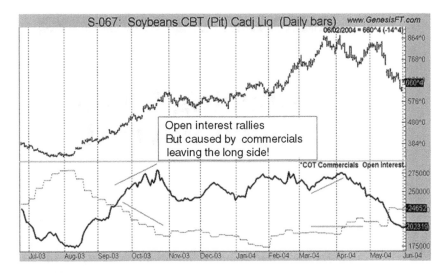

FIGURE 9.1 Soybeans Chart
Source: Genesis Financial Technologies, Inc. (www.GenesisFT.com).

My next presentation, Figure 9.2, is of the second soybeans chart in that same chapter, except this time I have added the dotted line showing what the commercials were doing. As you may recall, we saw a large increase in OI in April 2001, with prices in a steep downtrend. Traditionally this is supposed to be bearish. In this case it was not. Now we know why.

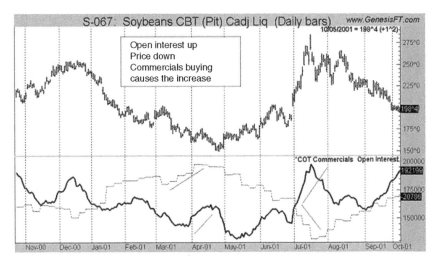

FIGURE 9.2 Soybeans Daily Chart
Source: Genesis Financial Technologies, Inc. (www.GenesisFT.com).

We can see from Figure 9.2 that while OI increased it was caused by the commercials going long ... in the face of the supposed weakness. Smart, informed money accounted for this increase, not the public or large traders. I'd also like to call your attention to the July 2001 time when there was a large increase in OI on a price rally.

As you recall this is supposed to be bullish, but in this case the rally quickly gave way to a top. No great surprise to us. We saw that at the same time the commercials' line was declining, meaning they were selling short, so there must have been a great deal of public and large trader buying, a symptom of a top. Again we see that looking inside OI tells us so much more than looking at just OI and price.

OPEN INTEREST DOWN, PRICE DOWN CAN BE BULLISH

A common view is that OI down on lower prices is bullish (see Figure 9.3). But the giveaway to this pattern is to note that the commercials were increasing their long positions on the decline in OI as I have marked off. The hefty decrease in OI means that the only buy orders coming in (new trades) were from the smart guys while the large and small traders were selling short or decreasing their bullishness by not buying.

Again, our inside view of the inner workings of the marketplace reveals what's really going on here, and in this case the OI decline is bullish.

Also note that in November of 1995 OI decreased on a decline in price,

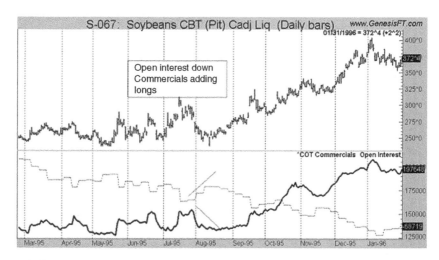

FIGURE 9.3 Soybeans Chart
Source: Genesis Financial Technologies, Inc. (www.GenesisFT.com).

but when we put on our X-ray goggles we can see that the commercials were adding to the long side in the middle of the month, just before a blast-off to the upside.

SOME REAL TRADES

I'd like to show you some real trades I have had based on this observation of price, OI, and volume. The trades I'm showing here were actually on my hot line, so these are not "after the facts were known" trades. The first, Figure 9.4, is lumber in the late summer of 2004 when prices had been in a large rally with an increase in OI. As you know, that is supposedly bullish. However, here the commercials were increasing their short positions (the dotted line). Heck, they just about were the total short position, and down came lumber (price).

Shortly after this decline lumber staged a nice trading rally with an opportunity to make more than $5,000 on a $1,500 investment in less than 40 days. Is there anything that might have tipped us off to such a potential up move? Most certainly. The commercials became very heavy buyers. As Figure 9.5 shows, they increased their long position (here the dotted line shows just their longs). As we can see, while OI dwindled, the commercials' long position was greatly increased, suggesting a rally was nearby. And it sure enough was!

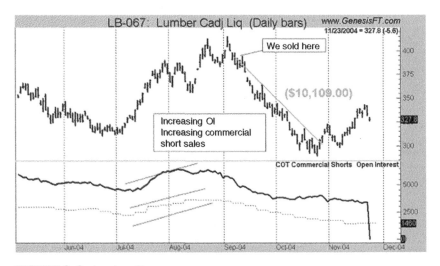

FIGURE 9.4 Lumber Chart
Source: Genesis Financial Technologies, Inc. (www.GenesisFT.com).

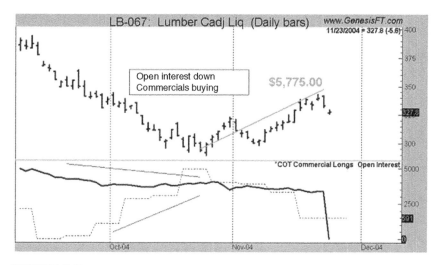

FIGURE 9.5 Lumber Daily Chart
Source: Genesis Financial Technologies, Inc. (www.GenesisFT.com).

This example was from real trading. It's not that hard to find opportunities such as this, week in and week out, during the trading year. Watch my Larry Live videos at www.ireallytrade.com and you will see me post many more opportunities.

Stocks and the Commercials

Our next chart to study (Figure 9.6) shows market action leading up to the flashy rally that lifted stocks to new highs in 2004, supposedly due to the reelection of George W. Bush. Was the reelection what really caused the rally, or was that just a convenient explanation? I'd say it was the latter because, as the chart shows, the commercials had been heavy buyers of the declining market. Ironically enough, OI was increasing during the decline, a supposedly bearish sign, but not so in this case.

What to Look for in Silver

I hope by now you are seeing what really moves the markets. With what you have learned so far, let's look at a chart of silver from 1998 (Figure 9.7). I have marked off times when the commercials have increased their short selling on market rallies—a real setup for short selling.

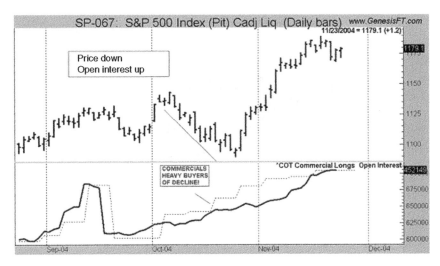

FIGURE 9.6 S&P 500 Index Chart
Source: Genesis Financial Technologies, Inc. (www.GenesisFT.com).

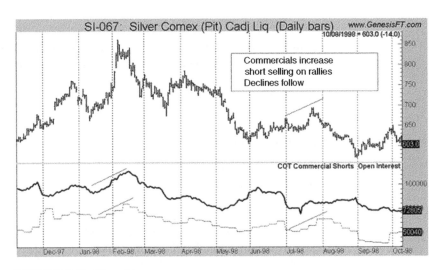

FIGURE 9.7 Silver Chart
Source: Genesis Financial Technologies, Inc. (www.GenesisFT.com).

A Golden Opportunity

Gold may well be one of the more responsive markets to the COT data. Let's look at two very nice buy points in 2004 when the commercials were heavy buyers while at the same time OI was low or declining rapidly. Again, what that tells us is the public is out of the picture. That's why OI is declining or low while at the same time the commercials have been buying. Such setups usually precede a rally and, more often than not, one of real consequence to a speculator.

In this case (Figure 9.8), notice how in early September of 2004 OI was dwindling while the commercials were buying right into the price weakness. Were they worried about the decline in price? Hardly; they met it face-to-face with a pickup on their long positions. That gave way to a rally with the possible profits of more than $5,000 per contract.

Then again at year-end 2004 gold broke and broke sharply—no surprise to us. In the latter part of November OI had increased and the public had become buyers while the commercials left the dance floor. Around the middle of the month the commercials did hear some music to dance to and stepped up their buying while OI declined—just the pattern we like to see—and away went gold one more time.

FIGURE 9.8 Gold Chart
Source: Genesis Financial Technologies, Inc. (www.GenesisFT.com).

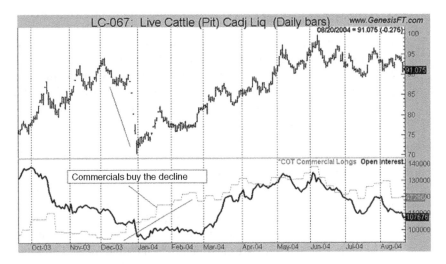

FIGURE 9.9 Live Cattle Chart
Source: Genesis Financial Technologies, Inc. (www.GenesisFT.com).

Mad Over Mad Cow Disease

I'll wrap up this chapter with a classic case of the commercials versus the great unwashed, misinformed public. At the start of 2004 one cow was suspected of being infected with mad cow disease in the state of Washington. The fear this disease would sweep across the nation like a wildfire on the prairies broke cattle prices in December 2003 and January 2004. On the surface things looked bleak for the entire industry.

We know that the surface of the water does not tell us what's really under the water. Hence, at that time, I turned my attention to the commercials, and as you can see in Figure 9.9, they became very heavy buyers amidst the mad cow sell-off. That could/should mean only one thing: cattle should move higher because the powers that be wanted to buy cattle and the commodity was in short supply.

While the news media was reporting that no one would eat beef anymore and had all but pronounced the industry's demise, the commercials were heavy buyers of cattle. As a speculator, had you gone long or bought cattle in January you could have made close to $11,000 for every $400 you put up—a nice return on your investment, thanks to knowledge, knowledge of the commercials.

CHAPTER 10

A Unified Theory of COT Data

It's all very well in practice, but it will never work in theory.

It's time to start to put the pieces together to fully understand the "Commitments of Traders" (COT) reports and create an indicator we can use—one that encompasses what we have come to know about the commercials, large traders, and small speculative traders. Heretofore, the industry has simply looked at the net commercial position or used the three-year look-back index discussed in Chapter 4. It is now time to go beyond these indicators and take a step forward.

What I have found to work better than the old indicators is to look at the commercials as a percent of open interest (OI), as opposed to just looking at the commercials versus themselves. We want to look at them versus all market action. Thus when OI is increasing and it is the commercials doing the increasing by adding short sales, a market peak should be close at hand, and vice versa.

Let me introduce this with a trade setup I saw, and wrote about for the leading financial paper in Japan. What you are about to read was written the last week of November 2004. Not a word has been changed. This is exactly what traders all over Japan read in early December 2004.

While the forecast is interesting, please pay attention to the indicator explained, as we will be doing more work with it.

The Future of the Japanese Yen

Businessmen as well as speculators are wondering what will happen next in the yen, and for the most part, are basing their conclusions on guesses and hunches while there is lots of information we can turn to.

This month I'd like to look at two very helpful tools that are telling us the yen is most likely going to experience a flat to down market, with a rally coming next February.

How can I possibly know this? Ahh, from a study of the past, and while the past does not perfectly forecast the future, it usually provides an excellent road map of what to expect.

One such road map is the seasonal pattern of the yen. Typically, its major up and down moves have come about the same time each year. This is largely due to the need to hedge against the U.S. dollar when most foreign contracts are drawn up. While there is a season as to when rice is planted and harvested, there is also a "season" as to when importers and exporters do most of their business and thus need to take action in the currency markets.

Let me show you what I am talking about with [a] weekly chart of the yen [Figure 10.1], under which I am showing the seasonal pattern that repeats year after year in the yen based on the last 27 years of trading in this currency. The index is the average price move for every nth day/week of the year over the data history (futures use Close – Close.1, stocks and indexes use Close/Close.1) on a centered basis.

The Seasonal Trend Index teaches us that the yen is usually weak and declines during the first part of every year. This is an observation I first made in my 1973 book on seasonal patterns in the

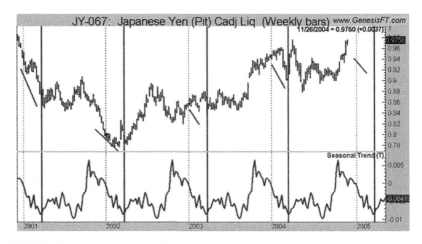

FIGURE 10.1   Japanese Yen Chart
Source: Genesis Financial Technologies, Inc. (www.GenesisFT.com).

marketplace [How Seasonal Factors Influence Commodity Prices, *Windsor Books*]. *As you can see, the years 2001–2004 followed pretty much in step with this pattern of first of the year weakness, and I see no reason this will not take place in 2005 as well.*

As a trader, however, someone who actually makes a living from speculating, I know I need more than just one tool, just a seasonal indication.

So let's next turn our attention to the smartest players in the business, the large banks, financial institutions, and corporate conglomerates that also make their living from correctly hedging in the currency markets.

Lucky for us, once a week they have to—are required by law to—disclose the amount of buying and selling they have been doing. This information is released in the Commitments of Traders report by the United States government. As you can well imagine, I closely follow what these superpowers of the world do each week.

As it stands now in the first of December they have been selling the yen and at a pretty good clip, something usually associated with market declines in the yen to dollar relationship.

A NEW INDICATOR—COMMERCIALS VERSUS TOTAL OPEN INTEREST

It's time to put much of this into perspective. We have learned that the commercials are the driving force of the market. We have also seen that high and low levels of OI have forecasting values and that there are parts and counterparts to OI, as well as that we need to open it up to see what the commercials are doing, to find out who is responsible for the increases and decreases in the valuable data.

One such way of breaking this down is to look at the commercials as a percent of total OI (commercial long position/total OI). This indicator provides some of the much-needed insight into the lore of the COT reports. For example, the commercials may not be carrying much of a long position. Let's say they are long 1,000 contracts while OI is 5,000 contracts, telling us that the commercials have 20 percent of the longs. Yet at another time the commercials are found again to be long 1,000 contracts, but total OI has now grown to 20,000 contracts. Right away we can see the increase in OI was not caused by the commercials! They have the same number of longs in both instances, but in the first case they have 20 percent of the action, while in the second case they have only 5 percent of the market!

This index, COT longs to total OI (CL/OI), allows us to place all of this into the correct perspective. The other side of this index would be commercial shorts to total OI (CS/OI), which shows when the commercials' shorting levels are high. Make no mistake about it. I still look at the charts to see the flow of total OI and the commercials as presented in the preceding chapters. I think this is a good practice, a good way to see what is going on and get a feel for the markets.

Let's take a look at this new indicator. The chart in Figure 10.2 looks at the short selling—selling in expectation of lower prices—that this group has done over the past nine years in the yen. It looks at their short selling as a percent of total OI in the market.

The telling point is that when the short selling by this group has mounted to 55 percent or more of all market action, longs and shorts, by all other market players, a top has been close at hand.

This certainly makes sense. When the smart money puts on an extreme position, controlling almost 60 percent of all market positions, and on the short side, it is no wonder a market is soon to decline. The history of the yen proves no exception to this rule. Look for yourself.

I have marked off with vertical lines when the commercial short selling to total OI ratio has exceeded 55 percent. Study this closely and judge for yourself. What I see is that the yen usually declines following such aggressive selling on the part of the superpowers.

As this is written, the last week in November 2004, I find the commer-

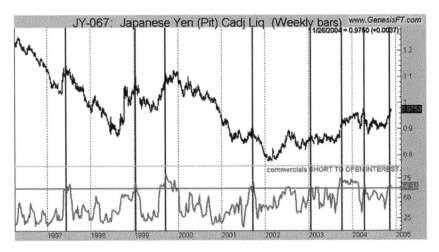

FIGURE 10.2 Japanese Yen Weekly Chart
Source: Genesis Financial Technologies, Inc. (www.GenesisFT.com).

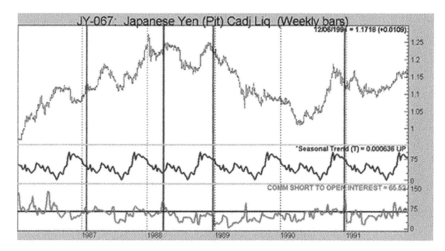

FIGURE 10.3 Japanese Yen Chart
Source: Genesis Financial Technologies, Inc. (www.GenesisFT.com).

cials' short position accounts for 64 percent of the total market OI. Clearly, no arguing about it. These guys are expecting a decline.

Notice that this comes at a time when we would also anticipate a seasonal break in the market, thus doubling the effect that one would expect here. We have confirmation of the seasonal pattern from the actual selling record of the smart money!

This is the way to market profits: to combine several major indicators, and to get them in conjunction with one another. Does the approach work?

Let's go back to 1988, a long time ago, to see what was happening as 1988, 1989, 1990, and 1991 opened up to the new year. In Figure 10.3, I have marked off with the vertical lines when the index was greater than 65 percent and, this is important, the seasonal pattern was suggesting a top should be close at hand.

The lesson from back then is equally clear. Large commercial selling as the new year dawns is highly predictive of a market top.

CALLING THE LOWS

What's good for the goose should be good for the gander. By this I mean the opposite situation should set up good buy points. What we look for here is the combination of a potential seasonal low while at the same time

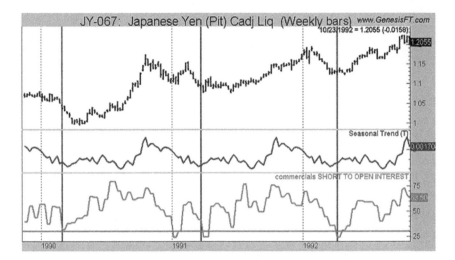

FIGURE 10.4   Japanese Yen Chart
Source: Genesis Financial Technologies, Inc. (www.GenesisFT.com).

the commercial ratio of commercials' shorts to total OI is very small. This tells us that they are buyers, not sellers, that in their infinite wisdom they do not think prices will be going lower. And more than just thinking this thought, they have bet on it, voted on it with large sums of money—large sums they acquired by being smarter than the market.

Figure 10.4 shows just this. I have marked with vertical lines times early in the year when the seasonal low was due. Typically the yen makes a low in the middle of March. That's been the case in most of the years under study.

So, if as we get into late February to March and see the commercial short ratio has dropped below 30 percent, we know that they are afraid to sell, that they have been buyers and we, ourselves, should consider that side of the market.

One picture, one chart says it all.

THE MORAL OF THE STORY

The lesson to be learned here is that there is power in a synergistic approach to speculating. By combining several good tools we greatly increase our ability to be successful in the art of speculation.

There are other tools that one might use—perhaps the relationship of the yen to gold, the yen to the U.S. dollar or to interest rates. But for now, what I see is a top forming in the yen and we will be looking for a buy come late February ... if the commercials have become buyers and stopped the aggressive short selling we see going on at this time.

PIECES OF THE PUZZLE

One man's floor is another man's ceiling.

We are faced with a problem as we delve into the COT readings of the commercials. It is this: do we monitor their long positions or their short positions? As I've shown in the prior chapters, it appears that either side of the equation can be used. The resolution is easy. Let's use *both* their buying and selling!

What I mean by this is that the best view can be garnered from taking the net long/short position of these wise men and putting that into the perspective of OI with the following formula. I have it in my Genesis software.

Stochastic Custom (COT Commercials/Open Interest, vara)

What the formula is doing is taking a stochastic of the net of commercial longs minus shorts divided by the total open interest of the last many weeks. (*Vara* is computer talk for a variable). You can play with this variable a great deal to see what number of weeks you think works best. While it varies from time to time and market to market, I have come to believe that, all things considered, a 26-week window to take this measurement is the best, across the board. In the old days, as I have discussed, we used a three-year look-back. In this day and age of volatile markets, though, a world full of fast changes and instant news, I have defaulted to the 26-week or one-half year window to get our perspective on how the commercials have been investing their money.

With that in mind, let's look at some examples of what I call WILLCO, short for Williams Commercial Index. In all the remaining charts in this chapter we are now using the total commercial short position divided by OI and using a 26-week measure. Some points should be made, though. Do not expect the index to be perfect.

Do expect it to generally point the way to important market reversals, to show us when a trend is most likely to end. The commercials are trend enders. Sometimes they do buy or sell early, but take heart, do not be discouraged, because our game plan is to wait for the trend of the market to get in phase with what the commercials' position is forecasting. When

WILLCO gets bullish, this means that we look for trend changes to go long and vice versa for selling or selling short.

Let's go back to the yen and see how this new index looks against the yen in 2003–2004. Figure 10.5 is quite a picture of how astute this crowd of investors has become. At virtually every major low of this time period we see the index rising above the buy trigger zone of 75–80.

Following just this indicator should have been a very profitable experience for even a beginning trader. The only weakness seen here is that there were some sell setups that took place prior to the market actually topping, such as that seen in late 2003. The crack at the end of 2004 was one of those things of beauty. Across the entire market the commercials had become sellers of gold, silver, and non-U.S. currencies, and then one day, December 7, 2004, these markets melted down. *Wall Street Journal* headlines expressed surprise at the decline. The proverbial gold and silver bulls were in shock; they had expected an ever upward and onward bull market. To them it made no sense. All the pessimistic elements that were in place at the start of the rally were still in place. There was no economic change. The war in Iraq was not getting better, or worse. How was it possible that their dream child could stumble at a time like this?

There was not a newspaper in the world that spoke in advance of a potential break on the precious metals. Far from it; the papers of the day had been extolling the power and strength of the rally. What a shock it was to trend followers, gold bugs, and news hounds.

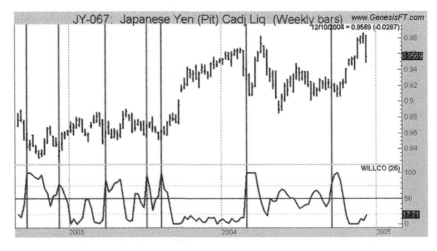

FIGURE 10.5 Japanese Yen Chart
Source: Genesis Financial Technologies, Inc. (www.GenesisFT.com).

The decline certainly came as no surprise to anyone who had been following the commercials.

I had warned subscribers to my newsletters of the impending decline of prices, as had virtually all of the other guys who have learned about this tool (I think most of them learned it from me and have added their twists and turns). Longtime friend and follower of this data Steve Briese (insidercapital.com) was resolutely bearish, telling his followers exactly what did happen. Floyd Upperman (wizkidtrading.com), George Slezak at commitmentsoftraders.com, and Jason Goepfert (sentimenttrader.com) had also alerted their subscribers of the impending break. Jason and Steve have done some great work on stock indexes by adding all the commercials' positions from all the various markets into one index to represent all commercial interest in all stock indexes, from the dumpy Nasdaq to the prestigious Dow 30.

These comments from Jason written on December 11, 2004, are insightful.

Perhaps notable, then, is that when looking at the total nominal value of outstanding positions in the full and E-Mini contracts for the S&P, Dow, and NDX futures, commercial traders are $38B net short, while nonreportables are at $30B net long. Only one other occurrence in history comes close to this large of a discrepancy in absolute dollars, the week ended 03/06/01. The S&P subsequently lost 14%, and the NDX lost 32% over the next few weeks. The next-closest is probably 03/12/02, which led to the wicked drop that summer.

It was certainly not shocking to us, to a lot of us. Indeed, it was rewarding. Here's an e-mail from one of my followers who has been a long-term bull on silver. He was able to sidestep the break thanks not to me, but to what the WILLCO was so clearly saying.

I really want to thank you for suggesting I [get] out of silver at $7.84. . . . As you well know it dropped to $7.00 and may drop further. My COMEX account is inordinately and irrationally important to me because it's just me and Mr. Market.

We lost a quarter million this month on the stocks but that's all right in the long run. ARE YOU GOING TO BUY SILVER? Or were you just happy to short it? You made an overnight fortune on your short obviously. I'd like to get back in at $7.00, but you remember just recently silver went from something to $8.30 to $6.30.

Thanks again. I would really be unhappy if I had woken up to a $10,000 loss. R.M.

FIGURE 10.6   Silver Chart
Source: Genesis Financial Technologies, Inc. (www.GenesisFT.com).

With that in mind, let's see what I was looking at back then. Here's that chart, Figure 10.6.

AN ANALYSIS OF SILVER

The vertical lines mark off where the major highs came in silver. Follow them straight down and you'll see that's when WILLCO was telling us that as a percent of OI the smart money bets were on the downside. The logical question is how you were able to get in. Was there any information to confirm the trade, to say, "Now, get in and sell short right here"?

Yes, there was. Lots of indicators were saying it was time. One I have taught and lectured about for years is a measure that I call ProGo, as it measures what I think the professionals are doing in a marketplace. Notice, if you will, in Figure 10.7, that while silver was rallying, this index (which shows just the buying by professionals) indicated that they were not following the rally. As silver went to new highs the index diverged, failing to make a new high on the entire rally.

The formula for the index is quite simple. It is the net difference between the open and close of each day averaged for the last 14 days. We will look more at this index on other charts, but for now I'd like to show you how to construct it.

FIGURE 10.7 Silver Chart
Source: Genesis Financial Technologies, Inc. (www.GenesisFT.com).

Many, many years ago I wrote about how to separate public buying from professional buying. The essence of the technique was to create an accumulation/distribution (A/D) line for the public that shows the change from yesterday's close to today's open. The professional A/D line is then constructed by using the change from today's open to today's close. Those two lines clearly tip us as to what is really going on. One line represents the public, as they cause the action from last night's close to this morning's open. The sudden change in prices, the gap from one day to the next, I think, is a reflection of what the public is doing. They read something in the paper, get goosed by talking heads on television or some likely inane news from the night sessions around the world, and make a rush to judge those results in their orders coming in before the market opens—thus causing the disparity of price change from last night's settlement to today's open.

The other side of that coin is that the change from today's open to the close today captures what the professionals did in the market. I see it like this. A market opens, then gets attacked by floor traders along with full-time traders, professionals like myself, while the public goes about their tasks and jobs for the day. We are the driving daily force and if a market closes above the opening of the same day, I think it means that we professionals rallied it to the close, even if it closed down for the day.

The public sees the market in a window of time from one day's close to the next day's close, while professionals see the market from today's opening to today's close.

Public Buying Defined

I take this one step further by simply constructing an index of the previous close to open (+/– values) for the public and then taking a 14-day average of these values. If today's open is greater than the prior close, the amount of price change is positive. If the open is less than the prior close, the value is negative.

Professional Buying Defined

Professional buying is arrived at by simply constructing an index of the price change from today's open to today's close (+/– values) and then taking a 14-day average of these values. If today's close is greater than the open, then the amount of price change is positive. If the close is less than the open, then the value is negative, even if the price closed higher than it did yesterday.

There are many ways to use this index. It can be a good entry tool and a great way to look at trend, but the main way I use it is to find divergences between price and professional accumulation and distribution. The silver chart in Figure 10.6 is a decent indication of such divergence, where price rallies and looks really strong to the public who just looks at charts. But pros like me, and now you, can see the huge divergence that from October 8, 2004, the professionals, at least as I measure them, were getting out. They were unwilling to buy as new highs were made on the rally. This is unusual. Good market rallies occur with an increase in professional buying, not a decrease.

As silver rallied to new highs I was alerted to the potential for a great selling juncture, first by WILLCO, then from the divergence between ProGo and price itself. All that was left was an entry. Here's what I used.

As shown in Figure 10.8, I drew a trend line using the two most recent short-term lows and planned to use that as my entry point, thinking that if prices went below the trend line I probably had a shot at a good short position. Let's get this straight. I did not know for sure. All trades have risk. What I wanted to do was slant the tables in my favor. I would not use a trend like this at all times for a sell. I used it here only because there was a very bearish setup in the market.

On December 7, 2004, the trend line was violated with an open below the trend line and my sell was executed. They don't all work out this way; please don't think that. But enough of them do to pay off the ones that don't! Had you not gotten in when I did, you could have—should have—sold on the opening of the next day. Now let me tell you, that would have been hard to do, though, as prices dropped so much. Yet that's what should have been done. Professionals sold there, while the public waited

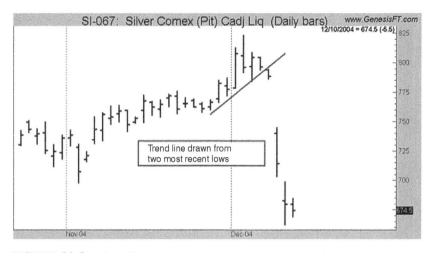

FIGURE 10.8 Silver Chart
Source: Genesis Financial Technologies, Inc. (www.GenesisFT.com).

for a bounce or pullback. There are very few hard-and-fast rules in this business of speculating, but one is that what everyone waits for will never happen.

GOLD, THE PROS, AND THE COMMERCIALS

In the spring of 2004 the reverse of all this took place on the gold market, as a very good sell point developed in mid-May. The setup is shown in Figure 10.9 and consists of WILLCO poking its head above 90 percent, telling us that the commercials owned most of the OI and that we should be looking for a rally to spring forth. An internal look at ProGo shows there is a large divergence between the decline in price during May while the professional line of accumulation climbs steadily uphill, a sure sign professionals were buying into the weakness. Price down and ProGo up is what I look for to say that the time is near.

The setup is pretty clear; the question that remains is when to buy, the exact day, time, and price. Again I would turn to simple trend lines. This business does not need a great deal of fancy math and long-winded formulas. Price is going up or down, and usually the best way to see that is to look at price; it speaks loudly. This is not rocket science stuff with equations, Bayes' Theorems, Bernoulli trials, and regression of linear analysis.

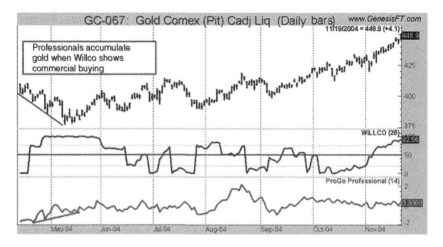

FIGURE 10.9 Gold Chart
Source: Genesis Financial Technologies, Inc. (www.GenesisFT.com).

Price went up or down, and the general trend was reversed or it was not. This is not a complicated process.

What you see in Figure 10.10 is the full picture, commercial bullishness, professional buying, and two simple trend lines. Take your pick. Price getting above either of these is an indication that the downtrend may have ended, and the odds are high due to the professional/commercial

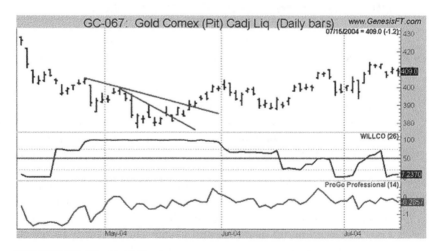

FIGURE 10.10 Gold Chart
Source: Genesis Financial Technologies, Inc. (www.GenesisFT.com).

setup. It was not a question of full moons or mystical chart patterns. By rallying up to the line that defines the current short-term trend, we can conclude that a trend reversal of some sort has taken place.

Trend lines are not to be used with complacency or callous disregard for conditions. No, these little gems of trend measurement have a time and place to be used, and by now you should be aware when that is. If not, either you are skipping through this book and should really go back to the beginning or you had better ask for your money back if you can't see how this all fits together as you are not meant to be a speculator.

Now that you have some ideas of how and when to get into a market, let's return to our study of the commercials by looking at some charts of WILLCO to drive home the importance of this setup tool. (See Figures 10.11 to 10.14.)

It is my hope these charts (see Figures 10.10 through 10.14) will help you understand that price rallies and declines do not just come out of the blue. Rather, they are the product or culmination of events that cause price action. One of the key elements of these events is what the smartest money in the business has been doing, not with e-mails and web pages like advisers, but with their cash. Cash is king, and the king rules.

One of the all-time great traders who went on to be an equally spectacular manager of money, Paul Tudor Jones, stated the object of what a trader is all about when he said:

"If you don't see anything, you don't trade. You take risk only when you see an opportunity."

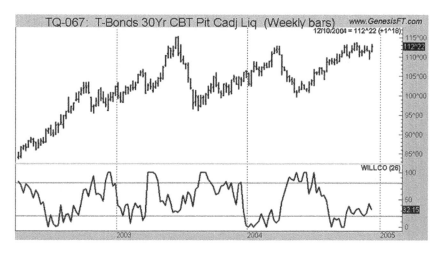

FIGURE 10.11 Treasury Bonds Chart
Source: Genesis Financial Technologies, Inc. (www.GenesisFT.com).

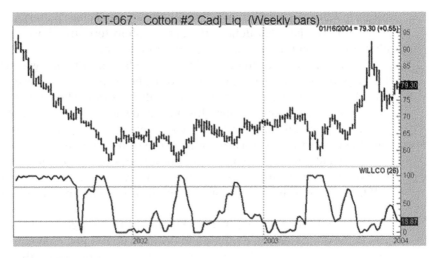

FIGURE 10.12 Cotton Chart
Source: Genesis Financial Technologies, Inc. (www.GenesisFT.com).

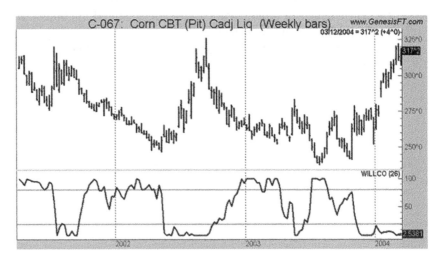

FIGURE 10.13 Corn Chart
Source: Genesis Financial Technologies, Inc. (www.GenesisFT.com).

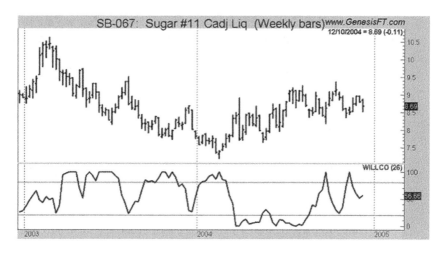

FIGURE 10.14 Sugar Chart
Source: Genesis Financial Technologies, Inc. (www.GenesisFT.com).

What the commercials and WILLCO do is help us focus on these opportunities, so we have a better set of odds when it comes to taking risk in the very risky world of trading. You see, most people get confused about trading and what this business is all about. There are so many emotions tied to this business. There is the emotion of making and losing money, and perhaps worse than the financial loss is the emotional loss from being proven wrong and having others—friends, lovers, and brokers—know about it. That's why I say, "What you think of my trade is none of my business."

The ultimate game or mental challenge is what we do—trade stocks and commodities. There is nothing else like it. We need skills, discipline, forbidden knowledge, a wad of cash, and total control of our emotions.

I'll get right to it. Often we trade, or respond to our trades, based on psychological factors, not financial ones. One that's tumbled me a few times—I assume you have run into it, or will shortly—is getting off track because of third party arguments.

In most relationships that go sour you will find a third party agitator (often undisclosed to one of the main parties). The same is true of our trading. In our case this problem can develop in one of two ways.

The first way, and what most often happens, is when we tell someone about our trade. That opens the doors to trader's hell.

Here's why. Once we tell someone else about what we are doing our ego is right there, flat out on the line. Ultimately we care more about our ego than our money, so we then begin a battle—an ego battle—to show the other person that we are right. There are many ways to wage this war, as I well know.

Many years ago I got into a public talking heads television on-air argument with Gene Inger, a fresh talent and the newest swashbuckler to hit the L.A. scene. He was bullish, and I was bearish . . . and worse yet, he was right.

Normally, I would have abandoned my bearishness and gone long. But since I'd spouted off my views on TV, who was I to leave them and be embarrassed? A fool, that's who I was! What he thought of my trades, and what Tinsel Town viewers thought of me or my position, suddenly became my business.

That's not the business I was in. I was in the buy low, sell high or sell high, buy low business. You'd never have known it. My "self" was on the line and when we speculators are on the wrong side of the issue we tend to dig in even more and not admit the errors of our ways.

Moral: telling others what you are doing will get you in more trouble than the markets.

The second way we get into third party arguments is to read, listen, think, or watch too much. We subscribe to someone's letter, read an e-mail blast, and then get into a confrontation, our view versus theirs. That's the nice thing about using the COT data: the data is more important than anything anyone on the telly will say or some astute cub reporter will divulge to you in the *Wall Street Journal* or *Investor's Business Daily*. Those fellows prattle away with gossip, rumors, and half-baked stories. There is no cash on the barrelhead in those reports, as there is with the COT reports. Again, cash is king and the king rules.

COMMERCIALS AND A LOOK AT SHORT-TERM TRADING

The debate about stock and commodity prices being random, and thus impossible to predict, continues in the hallways of academe while traders make the big bucks to fund grants for predicting what we are told we cannot.

I'll be the first to agree that there is randomness in stock and futures prices, huge chunks of it, in fact, tossed into the quagmire of price action every single day.

But, just because there is some randomness does not mean there is total randomness, just as some order does not rule out entropy.

Just don't tell that to an economics professor! He or she will fire back with the work of Maurice Kendall, a British math guy who in 1953 claimed prices "wander . . . almost as if once a week the Demon of Chance drew a random number . . . and added it to the current price to determine the next week's price" (as quoted in Stewart C. Meyers and Richard A. Brealy, *Principles of Corporate Finance*, McGraw-Hill, 2003, p. 347).

In *Principles of Corporate Finance*, we are told, "Today's price changes give investors almost no clue as to the likely change tomorrow." If that doesn't discourage you, keep right on reading and you'll find this lovely statement: "Prices in a competitive market *must* follow a random walk."

Why is this? If past price changes could be used to predict the future, investors could make easy profits, but their observation is that while investors take advantage of such patterns, price will adjust to their action; thus, "superior profits from studying past price movements disappear."

This is not good news, if true, for us struggling speculators. It means we cannot get a leg up in the game.

Yet, there are systems that have consistently made money. Hmmm . . . could Kendall and all these tomes of higher education be wrong? Yes, resoundingly yes! How can the Value Line or Zacks Investment Research selections, or even the lackluster Dogs of the Dow, have consistently outperformed the market? How is it possible my newsletter has been pretty consistent in making about $30,000 per year trading price patterns in the S&P 500? Luck doesn't last that long.

THE MARKET—IT'S NOT A FLIP OF A COIN

Here is my attempt to refute the adage that market movement is random, no more than a flip of a coin.

Flipping Out over Coin Flipping

Last week I read one of those anemic academic studies that conclude that the markets are totally random and you'd do better flipping a coin or throwing darts. Essentially, the author stated, the markets defy prediction, as there is neither rhyme nor reason to them.

Well, maybe. But my trading experience kinda slaps that idea in the face. You mean the millions of dollars I've actually made were all the product of luck? I'll be the first to admit some of the winnings were, but give me a break!

I fired up the old computer to look at this a little more closely, and some fascinating numbers popped up. First, it's pretty easy to show pork bellies or stocks are a flip of the coin—well, kind of. The first study I looked at was how many times the S&P 500 closed up or down for the day

TABLE 10.1 Number of Up and Down Closes

Number of up closes	2,762		
Number of down closes	2,507		
Strings of two up closes	1,366	Expected	1,381
Strings of three up closes	648	Expected	690
Strings of four up closes	294	Expected	345

since 1982. If it's a coin flip, then about half the days should have been up and half down. Taking that one step further, for every 100 heads there should be about 50 heads twice in a row, 25 three times in a row, 12 four times in a row, and so on. Table 10.1 shows what I found.

Hey, this looks pretty close to a coin flip! The biggest deviation is that we don't get runs of four up closes as often as chance tells us we should. Another interesting point is there are only four price bars or configurations possible each day, an up range (higher high and low), down range (lower high and low), inside bar (lower high and higher low), or outside bar (higher high and lower low). These were not equally distributed. There were 2,156 up range bars, 1,890 down range bars (13 percent fewer), only 565 inside bars, and just 592 outside bars.

Now, let's look a little deeper at the data because, as it's said, "Trend is the basis of all profits," not simply up and down closes.

It is the magnitude of the move that matters for us, not simply the fact that a market was up or down for a day. Now if the market is just a coin flip, then the price change from the open to the close should be about the same, regardless of whether we closed up or down. I find this is not the case. Table 10.2 reflects buying on the opening of the day after a string of consecutive down closes and exiting on the close that same day.

If we were dealing with just coin flips, the payoff should be about the same, regardless of the number of consecutive heads or tails. Well, that is simply not the case here, by a long shot. So much for a college education (I'm not down on education, have a few degrees myself and too many kids

TABLE 10.2 Consecutive Down Closes

Number of Consecutive Down Closes	Number of Trades	Profit on Next Trade
1	2,507	−$165,990
2	1,119	−$ 46,618
3	480	$ 38,563
4	182	$ 93,210
5	59	$ 56,783

still in college). What we know is that there is a huge bias for larger rallies when the market has experienced strings of consecutive down days.

It gets better than this when we turn our attention to real-time trading models. If, as the professors claim, the market is random, then a system should not work—the future they say is totally unpredictable—so systems' results should also put on quite a display of randomness.

PATTERNS TO TRADING PROFITS OR RANDOMNESS?

Let's now turn our attention to a trading system, one that trades the S&P 500. This is far from the best system I have. There are better ones, so randomness should be more visible here. I'll leave the specific performance results out for now, instead choosing to focus on the trade sequence shown in Table 10.3.

If we were dealing with total randomness, following the one winning trade sequence of 622 trades we should see that split in half to about 311 instances of two winning trades in a row. Instead we see 507. Half of 507 should give us about 253 instances of wins three times in a row. However, the data shows we get 412, and on it goes.

And again, more important and intriguing, is that the more winning trades we have in a row the larger the average profit per trade becomes.

The adages of "stay with the trend" and "when you're hot you're hot" are proven out here, and in other studies I have done, time and time again.

LOOKING AT LOSSES

A study of the losing sequences shown in Table 10.4 is equally fascinating in that it also reveals that either we are able to beat randomness or it does not exist.

TABLE 10.3 Winning Sequence

Consecutive Wins	Number of Trades	Next Trade Wins	Average Win
1	622	81.5%	$1,308
2	507	81.3%	$1,377
3	412	80.1%	$1,481
4	330	80.9%	$1,530
5	267	79.0%	$1,607
6	211	77.7%	$1,790
8	126	77.8%	$1,738

TABLE 10.4 Losing Sequence

Consecutive Losses	Number of Trades	Next Trade Wins	Average Win
1	159	77.8%	$1,101
2	44	72.3%	$1,059
3	12	58.3%	$1,151
4	5	60.0%	$1,497

Again the data speaks, and rather clearly: there is not an equal distribution of losses. The 159 losers should be followed by about 80 strings of two losses in a row. Yet we find 44. Then when we should get about 40 strings of 3 (160/2 = 80, 80/2 = 40), we see only 12. We also see that the average profit per trade increases from $1,101 to $1,497. That's a 35 percent increase, and there is a steady increase in average profits following losing streaks. This defies randomness!

Which is my point: while the markets are full of randomness, they are not totally random. Hence they can be predicted—not with 100 percent success, thanks to randomness, yet . . . logic, rationale, and order exist in our trading universe.

CALLING UPON THE COMMERCIALS

The random walk school, and it's a large one, alleges that prior price action cannot give us a clue as to what tomorrow will bring, that the markets are so efficient that there is no advantage to be had.

I see a slight advantage in that, overall, the market rallies more often than it declines. In fact, had you bought on the open every day since 1982 and exited on the first profitable opening, you would have made $95,563 on 1,420 trades. The problem is that the drawdown of $210,955 is a little steep for most of us. Yet there is clearly a bias to the upside.

So while randomness prevails and we can't predict, for sure, whether tomorrow will bring a rally or a decline, we see a bias.

SPLASHING ICE WATER ON THE PROFESSORS

The commercials, the large hedgers, the users and producers of a commodity, have a great influence on future price action. If they are net long—on balance—prices should rally. When they are net short, prices are most apt to decline. That's my theory, at least.

Now, if we can prove that thesis, thereby showing that the markets are not totally random, we demolish the efficient markets theory. That's quite a task; the MBA and PhD crowd have been trying to do that for years.

I tried an interesting little test. I programmed my Genesis software to buy the S&P 500 on the opening each day only if the COT commercials index, using a six-month time frame, was less than 50 percent—in other words, over the past half year the commercials had been doing more selling than buying.

It's All about Results

The answer to this little study was fascinating. Since 1982 there were 846 days that fit the criteria. Had you bought on the next bar's opening you would have lost money overall (not much—$170). The drawdown was a staggering $209,755.

Now, had you gone long only when the commercials were long (i.e., the index was greater than 50 percent), the results are dramatically different.

Using the setup of COT index more than 50 percent produced far fewer trades, only 371, but the profits were $76,605 for an average profit per trade of $212! Wow, what a difference the commercials make in trading, suggesting the markets are not totally random after all. Check this out as well. The drawdown was only $39,145.

Never, ever would I trade just because the COT index was greater than 50 percent, but it's sure a great place to start.

"Maybe, just maybe," I hear you saying, "the S&P 500 is an exception." I wondered myself so I did the same study on Treasury bonds.

Again I had the computer buy only when the COT six-month index was less than 50 percent. The results were 633 trades that lost $13,985 with a $25,733 drawdown. In short, it was not a good setup for buying, vis-à-vis the same thing in the S&P 500.

The next query was to buy when the COT index was greater than 50 percent. What I found is illuminating. There were 606 trades making a profit of $28,418 with a mere $17,695 drawdown.

Killing Two Birds with One Stone

These tests are pretty conclusive. Both markets were more predictable and profitable to buy when the commercials were long, and predictably bad to buy when the commercials were short. Clearly, there is an advantage to be had that is not already factored into prices, and we can attempt to capitalize on that advantage.

That's point one. The markets are not totally random.

Next, this little study validates the notion that the commercial position has a great impact on price performance, even on short-term swings in the marketplace. For years people have said that the commercial position has no bearing on future price performance. They can think that—the more the better, as a matter of fact—but the hard numbers expressed here are enough to convince me to continue keeping an eye on these guys.

CONFESSION TIME

They say confession is good for the soul, so this might be better for me than for you. Oh, I knew it would happen—2003 was sailing along so smoothly, life was good and trading was better, trade after trade. Me, my laptop, and a few S&P 500 patterns had made more than $400,000 for the year.

Sure, it was not a straight-up path to heaven. It had its twists and turns, but while the road had bumps, it was not rocky.

Until . . .

. . . In the middle of November, I went into a drawdown. While it was not a large drawdown, mere kid stuff compared to some I've had, at my age and with my supposed trading abilities, every drawdown is too large. Way too large. But that's par for the course. As a matter of fact, every year for the past 15 or so I've talked to myself (see what trading can do to you) about the eventual drawdown I would have. They are a yearly occurrence in this business, so you had better preframe yourself for them, as I had.

But this one was different. It wasn't the size of the drawdown that got to me. Naw, it was *me*.

There, I got it off my chest. This is hard stuff to talk about, but someone has got to talk about more than the easy money all those web pages banter about. So I'll continue.

For whatever reason, you see, I got off my path, off my system, in early November of 2003. Well, "whatever reason" is just me covering up. I know darn good and well what happened.

I got bearish.

Not wildly, end-of-the-world bearish; I just took on a negative bias toward stocks.

The Plot Thickens

Our state of mind is really two states or maybe types. Like most of you, I think and research the markets constantly. This is my passion. Nothing in my life has motivated me more than understanding and cracking the code(s?) of the markets. It has too often been all that I have lived for, to my loss—but let's never forget to my gain as well, and to the gain of those around me.

This conglomeration of market stuff was created with the rational mind. It took years of effort, trials, failures, and learning.

So of course I stopped following it and or tweaking it to support my bearishness. My November nemesis was not the system. It was another part of my mind.

Still, after all these years—41 years of staring at these stupid charts—my nemesis was me. It's almost as though I stalked myself like some cat hunting its prey . . . like the Jack London story of how Eskimos kill wolves.

THE TOUGHEST PART OF TRADING

It's not the markets, it's us. It is a lot like driving on California's fastest freeways. You know what? They are remarkably safe. But if for one instant you lose your focus, swerve, fail to heed the laws of sensible driving—you're a goner.

Have you ever been in a wreck? The first thought is, "Gee, if I had just left home five minutes earlier or later," or "Why wasn't I looking?" Stuff like that runs through your head.

As it does with trading. It takes only one bad decision to cause your crack-up. Mine was I figured the market was going to go down—because I wanted to buy at lower prices (I can hear you chuckling now). I was upset that I had not bought lower and kept waiting for prices to "come back to me." Yeah, right. I always thought my mother never raised any fools. No longer do I carry that spurious notion! I had become a hopeless fool trying to prove a point—*to be right when I was wrong.*

All it takes is one slight error. That's all.

There I was, using a pretty good little system developed by half my brain, but the other half got into this bearish thing and began tinkering with reality.

The system itself actually made a good deal of money during that time period, but not me. Nope, I gave some back based on my very intelligent bias and good hard thinking, most of which was based on trying to prove a point.

Big deal that I was not the only one. I read every newsletter that agreed with me, bought into the Fibonacci retracement argument, even looked at candlestick charts (that provided some comic relief for me—a chart chat room had a candelabra of commentators who could not agree on which candlestick pattern it was). Not that it matters . . . what matters is I fell asleep at the wheel and let my mind get carried away doing the talking and explaining without regard for reality.

What a waste a mind is. I would have done better using half of it than all of it! Whatever you "think" in this business is destined not to happen.

MORE ON THE MIND-SET OF A TRADER

It all starts in your mind. Even the idea of speculating begins there, deep down in one of those recessed creases you see in brains. Thus we'd better pay at least some attention to our mind-set or state if we are to succeed at this art of trading.

I'm No Expert, But . . .

While I've written on this subject, it's a stretch to claim I'm any sort of expert. Sure, my undergraduate minor was in psychology, but my database is not hundreds of winning traders. My database to study this phenomenon has been primarily me—and a ton of losing traders who call me every day, stop by to visit, or meet me at seminars.

I once interviewed more than 50 pretty good traders to see what made them tick along with 50 of the all-time worst traders I have ever known. The amazing thing is that there wasn't much difference in the basic belief system.

Both camps expressed a strong desire to win, both tribes of traders had positive work ethics (obsessive, if the truth were to be known), and both believed they would reign triumphantly.

There were two major differences that I was finally able to pin down. The first is that the big winning traders were quite funny, humorous, and I guess you could almost say carefree in how they approached winning and losing. You bet, they didn't like losing, but they dealt with it. The losers professed to hate losing as well, but were far more uptight about it than the winners. They were less accepting of the losses.

The winners rolled with the punches, while the losers were usually floored.

This was especially true with trading size. Small traders, whether winners or losers, stay that way because they can't mentally handle the idea of increasing the number of contracts they trade. Size matters, but the big winning traders never let the size of their position throw them off from doing the right thing. Small traders trying to get big get carried away with the size of the trade and thus cannot get out when they are wrong. Size causes mental stickiness for these people. The size of the trade does not matter, but when you do step up the number of contracts, maybe from one to two or from 10 to 50, don't change anything you have been doing because of the new level of commitment. After all, the market does not know—or care—how many contracts you have. The rules have not changed, and neither should you.

An even bigger difference between these polar groups was seen in how they used stop-loss protection. To a man and woman, the large successful traders had an absolute form of risk control, while the margin meeters were seemingly without a notion of protection. Their stop losses were invariably triggered by pain; when they were under more pain than they could manage, then and only then did they pitch their positions. The winners had reversed that old athletic canard of "no pain, no gain" to "with pain, no gain." They avoided pain, while the losers did not. It's as simple as that!

Here are some comments from one of Europe's most successful traders, Paul Rotter, known as the "Flipper," that may give you more insight into what it takes to be a winner at this.

I've experienced big losses, but have always been able to come back with a winning streak. So, I am no longer that sensitive about losses. I know that I can make them back. Because of this, I am more willing to stop trading on bad days and take small or medium losses.

One of my strengths is the ability to become more aggressive during winning streaks and to do the opposite during a losing streak. This goes against what most people do.

You should have a person who has nothing to do with trading who will turn off the trading terminal after a certain amount of losses and send you home; that would save traders thousands.

I am constantly adjusting my trading style to match specific market conditions. For example, on volatile days I generally put fewer orders into the market and execute more directional trades, although I mostly hold them for only a few seconds.

I always set strict daily targets and limits for my profit and loss. The most important element is the stop limit, or simply the size of the loss, which will cause me to turn off my trading screen. I try to liquidate my positions as soon as they start going against me.

A guru or analyst might have to stick to his opinion, but a trader should not have an opinion at all. The stronger your opinion is, the more problems one has when it's time to close a losing position.

The solution to all this is to get back on the correct side of the road as soon as you possibly can. In other words, give up your mind when you are wrong and get back to the reality of what matters: the commercials.

When you deal with numbers, readings of what the commercials are doing, you are dealing with an absolute, not some will-o'-the-wisp tale that you can't quite put your finger on or get all the data for. The COT data is bullish, bearish, or neutral, and any 2 or 20 of us looking at this data see the same thing. It takes no interpretation, no long-drawn-out discussion. It is or it isn't, and it's been a darn sight more reliable over the years than the *Wall Street Journal* stories or TV's prettiest talking heads.

Consider this series of questions I saw posed on a web site chat room where many high-powered speculators were comparing notes with one another regarding retail sales at the end of 2004.

> *It appears the figures are in, and consumer confidence has jumped to 102+ vs. 94 expected. The question is: why has the just recently completed Christmas shopping season been projected to be low, from a retailer's point of view, when consumers are so confident? Major sales going on at every retail level, with the possible exception of high-end items, to try to make this a good year for retail in the last week of '04 buying. Does the Conference Board look at a cross section of the shopping/working public, or do they look at just middle management and up?*
>
> *This also brings up the questionable "Durable Goods" report, which had an increase, and caused the markets to move up accordingly. Durable goods are big items that are expected to be around five years or more (washing machines, dryers, refrigerators, etc.). You can also throw in planes, trains, and cars. But, if durable goods are items that are going to be purchased only once in a long time frame, why are they so important that they cause the market to move so dramatically?*

Who could correctly answer all those questions, anyway? Certainly not me. These are questions that may be impossible to answer, or at least answer correctly, and even if answered correctly they don't help us get side by side with the powers that be, the smart money. Why fool around with the fluff? Let's cut to the chase. It seems a better and more direct question would have been, "What has the smart money been doing?"

We have no need to ask our broker, barber, or banker what he or she thinks. Who are they compared to the commercials, the greatest powers in the marketplace? They are a bunch of nobodies, that's exactly who they are. Their thoughts and opinions are those of the crowd, the public. I've tapped you right into the real players in these markets. So quit, right now, asking and looking. The truth is right here. It's as good as it gets in this business—far from perfect, but it is the best there is. What I'm trying to get at here is that no one—not me or anyone else—has the be-all and end-all answers to the markets. There is no perfection in this business. So stop wasting your time looking for the fountain of youth or market perfection. It will do you far more good to study the commercials. Realize they are usually a little early, so look for a price trend change, and finally, use their action in relationship to trend as I discuss in the final chapter.

CHAPTER 11

A New Twist on the Commercials

Using Them for Stocks

The only commercials in the stock market are for brokerage firms.

Okay, enough of this psychobabbling. Let's get back to work. For years I have tried to understand how the commercials act toward commodity prices. I know they buy on a scale down, sell on a scale up. In fact, years ago, when the data came out one month late, we tried to develop an estimate of their buying and selling. Guys like Lee Turnbull and myself along with Jimmy Murzyn and Bill Meehan went to work to see if we could create a synthetic form of this index.

While those early efforts were not successful, I think I may have finally cracked the code. Let's start with a chart of soybeans, Figure 11.1. In addition to price I'm showing directly underneath that my stand-in proxy for the commercials, my estimate of what they are doing. The bottom panel is the actual COT commercials index on a six-month basis. Both the commercials and the proxy have been marked off at 80/20 percent bullish/bearish levels.

I have marked off with the vertical lines just the times the proxy index entered the buy zone. While not a perfect fit, the proxy index usually moves step for step with the actual COT index. Here's another example. Look carefully at Figure 11.2 to see how closely the synthetic index models or assumes the general peaks and valleys of the actual COT index.

As you can see, most of the time the proxy and the COT index are in agreement on the buy or sell side. Well, if that's the case, that we've cracked the code, we should be able to apply this proxy index to stocks to

129

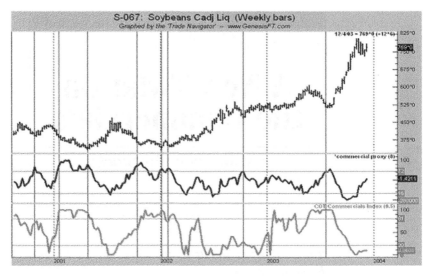

FIGURE 11.1   Soybeans Chart
Source: Genesis Financial Technologies, Inc. (www.GenesisFT.com).

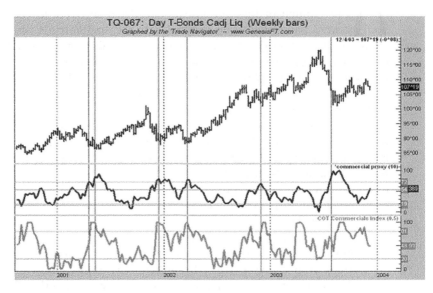

FIGURE 11.2   Treasury Bonds Chart
Source: Genesis Financial Technologies, Inc. (www.GenesisFT.com).

see what the commercials would do if they were in that market. What a help that could be! Since there is no reporting similar to what we have in the futures markets, if we could model commercial activity for stocks we'd have an insight, an advantage no one else in the game has. Here are several stocks of interest.

Keep in mind that even the commercials are not perfect. They may buy too early or sell too early, and sometimes they are just flat out wrong, but that is very rare. In Figure 11.3 the proxy index pointed to some good buys in Microsoft. Let's look at a few more (see Figures 11.4 through 11.6).

It appears we may have additional insight into individual stocks based on this measure, which I first introduced to my subscribers in 2003. Since then we have seen it win some and lose some, but there have been a lot more winners than losers with this idea. While I am not yet willing to fully reveal the index (don't worry, you can see it updated on my web site at www.ireallytrade.com), I'm more than willing to give a general explanation of the tool to you at this time.

The index was developed by seeing the consistency of commercials to buy weakness and sell strength. I've seen them do that for the past 30 years. All I've done here is take downside activity that occurs in an accumulation mode and assign that action to the mock or synthetic commercial proxy index. While the index can be applied to any stock and I also

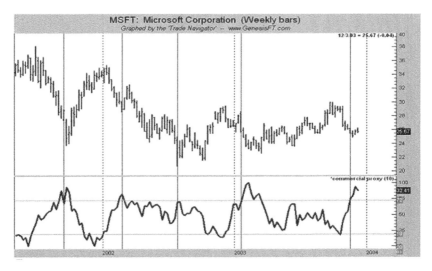

FIGURE 11.3 Microsoft Chart
Source: Genesis Financial Technologies, Inc. (www.GenesisFT.com).

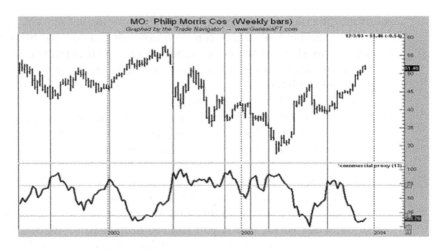

FIGURE 11.4   Philip Morris Chart
Source: Genesis Financial Technologies, Inc. (www.GenesisFT.com).

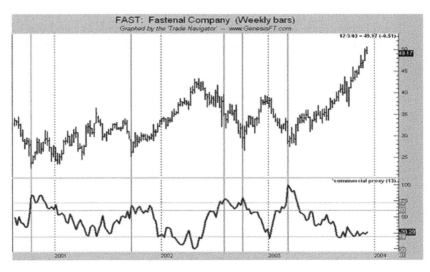

FIGURE 11.5   Fastenal Company Chart
Source: Genesis Financial Technologies, Inc. (www.GenesisFT.com).

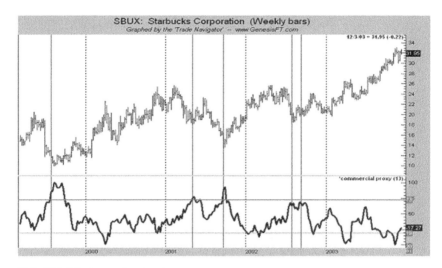

FIGURE 11.6 Starbucks Chart
Source: Genesis Financial Technologies, Inc. (www.GenesisFT.com).

use the same formula for my stock commentaries in Japan, China, and Europe, I think it works the best on quality stocks, not low-priced junkers. Nonetheless, I will display the index here (see Figures 11.7 through 11.10) on the more speculative issues as well.

This may prove to be a valuable tool for stock traders and investors. I also wanted to show these stock examples as I hope to do more with

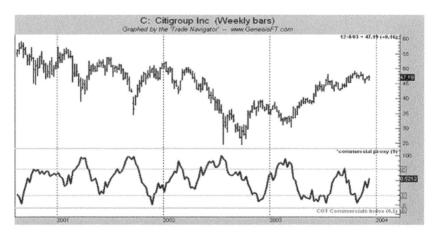

FIGURE 11.7 Citigroup Chart
Source: Genesis Financial Technologies, Inc. (www.GenesisFT.com).

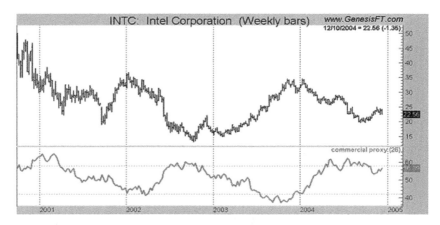

FIGURE 11.8   Intel Corporation Chart
Source: Genesis Financial Technologies, Inc. (www.GenesisFT.com).

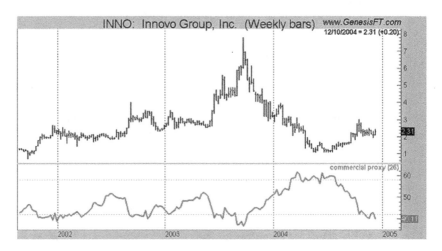

FIGURE 11.9   Innovo Group Chart
Source: Genesis Financial Technologies, Inc. (www.GenesisFT.com).

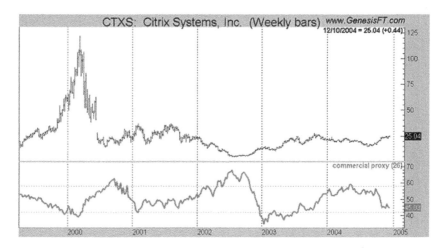

FIGURE 11.10 Citrix Systems Chart
Source: Genesis Financial Technologies, Inc. (www.GenesisFT.com).

this tool so it can help us tell more about what the COT report is probably going to say about commodities. In short, we now have a sneak preview before other traders, and a suggestion of what the COT index will be doing. There are several commodity markets that do not have COT data; pork bellies, the CRB index, and foreign markets come immediately to mind.

Now, thanks to the proxy index, we can have a sense of what the commercials would be doing and reporting, if we had reporting requirements in these markets.

CHAPTER 12

Pointers and Thoughts on Trading

Fear not those who argue but those who dodge.

If you don't learn to fall, you will never learn to fly. Trapeze artists and commodity traders have a great deal in common. We are both trying what few will attempt, and both seek a reward with unusually high risk. Sam Keen, in writing *Learning to Fly* (Random House, 1999), has produced a delightful read for trapeze artists as well as traders.

The fundamental principle of trapeze artistry is, "Learn the fall before the trick; prepare for failure." I can think of no greater counsel to provide traders. Most of us are so revved up to trade, to make a million, to do a triple somersault with a double twist, that we forget the risks we are taking.

Truly, until you learn the best way of failing or losing, which will surely happen to you as a trader, you will not be in the game long enough to become a winner.

Trapeze performers begin learning their trade rigged up in harnesses with spotters who are able to pull on ropes to protect them from injury. I'd call that paper trading.

From harnesses they matriculate to flying through the air, but with a net underneath them. The net is not a simple or sure thing. Landing in the net incorrectly can cause severe damage, so they practice landing in those nets, day after day. Their nets are like our stop-loss orders. Used incorrectly they can cause major problems, but used correctly they will save your financial and emotional life.

THE ART OF USING STOPS

This came hard to me in my early days of trading. I was forever doing spectacular aerial routines, the kind that grabbed national headlines and got me top billing. But, like the Wallindas walking tightropes, I had equally spectacular (at least to my antagonists) crashes.

Margin calls and I were no strangers; indeed, we were the best of friends. Initially I thought it was my dumb luck or lack of a better or perfect system. I now see that as fallacious. The fundamental rule of trading is that this is a very imperfect game. It has large chunks and gaps of totally random activity that no one can explain. It is indeed unpredictable.

Therefore, sad to say, it appears there is no magical place to put stops, no secret number or price zone that offers us protection from the unpredictable.

What Stops Protect

Stop-loss orders do not change the mechanics of the game. They cannot make a losing system a winning system. Their sole function is to act as that net under "fliers" to protect us from a crack-up. If you trade without stops, I assure you that at some point, and most likely soon, you will meet your trading demise.

The function of stops is to protect our dollars. Thus our stops should be based on the maximum dollars we will accept as a loss, not chart formations, trend lines, and the like. Stops do not protect us from trend lines. They protect us from losing money, so stops based on that—losing money—work the best.

It has been almost 20 years now since I have had a margin call—and yes, I do still trade, probably a couple of hundred contracts a week. What turned me around was the consistent use of stops. Plus, there's another great advantage to using stops, analogous to trapeze artistry: when you know there is a net underneath you, you have the liberty to try all sorts of fancy flying and new tricks of the trade.

THIS IS NOT A BLACK-AND-WHITE BUSINESS

"But you said . . ." "Page 63 says to . . ." "This line crossed that one . . ." "It's trading day of month 11; shouldn't I . . . ?" Those are typical comments I hear every day from readers of my books, and these illustrate an important part about being a winning trader.

It's Just Like Life

Not only is this business not black and white, neither is life. We all know that (I think), yet as traders we want absolutes so badly that we absolutely forget to think. It's just like math. Math is an absolute, but when applied to the imperfect world of stocks and commodities it reverts to being a tool that simply gives more clarity and definition to the imperfections. Please, never forget that above all else, speculation is a thinking business. If you are not good at thinking, or at least getting correct answers, I'd look for the off ramp if I were you.

The problem begins with a wish or hope that there is some be-all and end-all automatic/systematic approach to trading.

The two greatest bits of bad information so-called advisers and authors such as myself foist on the great unwashed masses are either extreme and continual bearishness or the belief that somewhere, someplace, there exists an absolutely perfect system, that there is precise cadence, order, and structure to the markets. These are the two great myths of speculation.

Yes, there are times to be bearish on stocks and the economy, but there's an entire camp of newsletter writers making a pretty good living by deliberately pandering to fears of gloom and doom, of another 1929 . . . starting tomorrow. I know these folks. I've appeared at the same symposiums with them, and I've seen them consistently bearish—in one case since 1962! One of these "Negative Nellies" in a private conversation told me that there was a huge market of investors who feared the future and actually believed things were falling apart quickly and it was his business to fan these fires. He added, "It's easier to sell subscriptions to these people. They are an easy-to-target market, and if I'm wrong on stock picks, it doesn't matter. Performance does not count. It's reaffirming their belief that they want to hear."

This crowd is full of pontificators, good people who have overanalyzed everything and concluded that the future for the United States and the world is behind us. What a bunch of crap. Even the most cursory study of history will establish one dominant fact: man's condition and lot in life are constantly getting better. Yes, there are some downs, but they are far outweighed by the ups.

There is another side to this coin, the "Cosmic Trader" who is convinced there is an explanation for every market high and low, that every uptick and downtick in price is fully explainable, and usually for a pretty stiff fee payable up front to them! When I was young and ignorant of the ways of the market and my fellow man, I fell for this pitch. After all, these people had a track record of success and could explain away all the previous market moves, those that had taken place in the past.

Usually the foundation for this belief is based on the legend of W. D. Gann. I've already written elsewhere that it was just a good dose of showmanship mixed with some winning trades, a bit of braggadocio, and an aggressive public relations man. Again this is not my opinion, but facts as related to me by F. B. Thatcher, the advance man for old W. D. Gann and his son.

The more time I spent in outer space with this crowd, the more losing trades I saw. While their explanations of the past were brilliant, their forecasts of the future were right only about 1 out of 20 times and, naturally, that's the one they talked (bragged) about in all their advertisements. There is no reality here. The fact that they were dead wrong in the past does not prevent them from again attempting to predict the future! Accuracy, making money, has nothing to do with their life. It's all about trying to prove that their mumbo jumbo works.

Of the thousands of traders applying this cosmic logic I've seen only two do well, Arch Crawford and Jerry Favors. Two out of thousands is not a great batting average, and Arch and Jerry are damn smart people, well-trained, experienced traders who use more than just one approach.

The bottom-line problem with the "all can be known" thesis is that it causes you to throw away fear, to place your convictions, and money, on a thesis, not what's actually going on in the market. If your focus is the market, what's happening now, and not a belief that stock or commodity prices must do something, your chances for success will skyrocket.

A perfect system or approach does not exist. It never has, and never will. The closest thing to the truth of what moves the markets that I have found is the commercials.

If there were such a thing as perfection in this business, then that would mean (1) the markets contain no random inputs, and (2) someone else would have already found the magical solution and own most of the free world by now. Since we know the markets do have a high degree of random influence from ever-changing news, weather, and traders' outlooks and that even the best traders and funds tap out, we must realize that the markets are not to be traded with a 100 percent mechanical approach. Things change.

Does this sound strange coming from someone who has spent just about his entire adult life developing systematic approaches to trading? Probably so, and it should not be taken to mean all my work, or systems and such, don't work.

The point I want to make is that *life is a judgment call, but that call is based on having data and systems to make life work better.* So it is with trading. I need a systematic approach to get me into and out of trades. I need absolute stops, and I sure as heck need precise entry rules.

But above all, I need to use some judgment of when to use this stuff. Let's look at an example from real life.

If you are driving down the road and a truck is dead ahead coming at you in your lane, do you stay in that lane or swerve across to the empty lane where you are not supposed to be? The rules and law are clear: you're not supposed to be over there. The system says don't do it, but reality is an 18-wheeler in your lane. Let's see, do we follow all the rules or do we adapt to the situation at hand? Survival is a function of adaptation.

Reality rules, on the road and in the markets. *The first rule of life is to survive. The second rule is that all rules can be broken if doing so supports the first rule.*

Speculation follows the same rules as life does; they are integrally the same. Successful trading is the art of using knowledge (systems) at the right time. This means when it's time to use the system or rule, you check for oncoming 18-wheelers. That's what thinking is all about.

To summarize, we do need systems for living and systems for trading. But it is not mandatory that we follow all systems exactly all the time. The reason is that systems do not adapt to any new bits of reality. That's what our mind is for: to observe, to record, to note changes, and then to develop an optimum use of the system.

If you do not know what to do as you are trading, you must follow the rules because they will keep you alive. If you like market conditions and they fit what your rules suggest, go for it. If the rules don't fit conditions or conditions don't fit the rules, pass. You don't have to trade every day.

The object of having systems and rules is to run them to your best advantage, and not to let them run you.

KNOW WHEN TO HOLD 'EM, KNOW WHEN TO FOLD 'EM

The paramount secret to making money trading stocks and commodities is learning how to hold on to winning trades.

It appears there is nothing easier than making money trading. The illusion is all you have to do is catch a big up move and then hold on until the price skyrockets to where the angels of speculation rule in the clouds.

Jesse Livermore said it best: "It was never my thinking that did it for me, it was my sitting that made me big money. My sitting! Men who are right and can sit tight are uncommon."

Sounds like pretty good advice, but you are probably thinking to yourself, easier said than done. Right? And, very, very easy to do in hindsight. Can hindsight give us a clue about trading into the future? Can it give us a strategy for sitting tight on big moves?

I think so, and would like to share with you some of my ideas about what to do once you get a big fish on the line. There is a game plan for holding on to big trades, but following the game plan is hard because:

- Our natural tendency is to take small profits to pay off recent losses.
- Our fear of losing profits exceeds our hope of holding on.

There they are, the reasons most people can't hold on. Let me plumb the depths of your mind a little more here. The pattern of taking quick profits (usually, as I said, to pay off recent losses) is emotionally dependent and is not supported by any sort of market logic. The market does not care about you or your recent wins and losses. A big trend move is not aware of you. There is no relationship between you and the trend. The two entities are not intertwined, so why act like they are?

Plus, what can best pay off recent short-term losses—a short-term gain or a megatrend move? The answer is obvious, the megatrend, so you had better learn to hold 'em.

The fear of losing profits is very powerful. We don't like to give back what we just got, so we take little profits. We are unwilling to sit through trading ranges of back-and-forth action—we want a "free-falling safe" type of market or a skyrocket. These do happen, but they are not the rule. The rule is large downtrends drop, bounce around in a trading range, then drop again.

Traders get spooked during the trading range and thus exit the major long-term move.

THE ABSOLUTE TRUTH OF INVESTMENTS

The truth is that it takes time for any small investment to become a big one. Time, and time alone, creates growth, regardless of whether it's a giant redwood, this year's soybean crop, our children, our business—or our trading positions. Seldom do huge profits come overnight (which is why massive, quick, explosive windfall moves should be exited quickly). Short-term traders never give the crop time to grow, and thus doom themselves to an unproductive crop.

There are two problems here. The first is that you must preframe your mind to recognize that major moves can have hefty pullbacks. You need to prepare your mind and emotions to realize this is the way the markets work.

Preframing

What a great word and concept! The idea is that if you preframe your belief system as to what the future will be like, you will be able to respond rationally—correctly—when the time calls for it. This is one of the most valid psychological concepts I have ever used.

At the start of every year I preframe myself to equity dips, to losing trades, by telling myself that at some point in the coming year I'm going to get beat up, badly most likely. I tell myself it may last a month or two, maybe even three, so when it does come I can deal with it.

When it comes to holding on to trades it's the same thing. Figures 12.1 through 12.4 depict some great trend moves. Look at them carefully and you will see that along the way there were some pretty steep antitrend rallies and declines. See, this is how the market actually dances, and we need to learn the dance to stay on the floor.

So How Is It Done?

This is the second problem, that of having a strategy or system that allows us to sit through these antitrend moves in order that our preframed mind has a framework of reference to respond to, not the emotions of fear and greed.

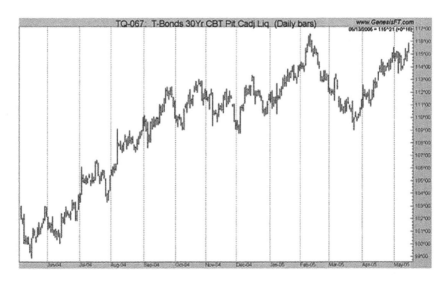

FIGURE 12.1 Treasury Bonds Chart
Source: Genesis Financial Technologies, Inc. (www.GenesisFT.com).

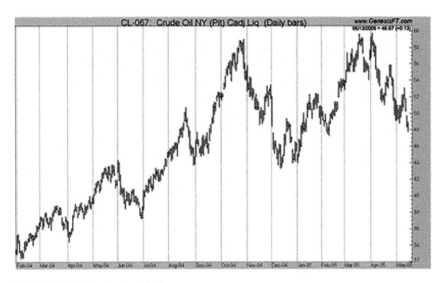

FIGURE 12.2 Crude Oil Chart
Source: Genesis Financial Technologies, Inc. (www.GenesisFT.com).

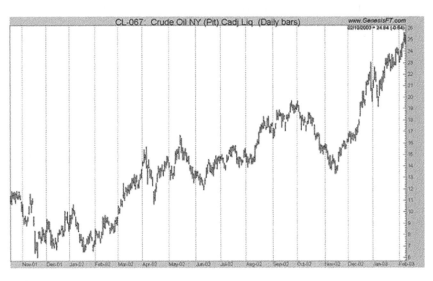

FIGURE 12.3 Crude Oil Chart
Source: Genesis Financial Technologies, Inc. (www.GenesisFT.com).

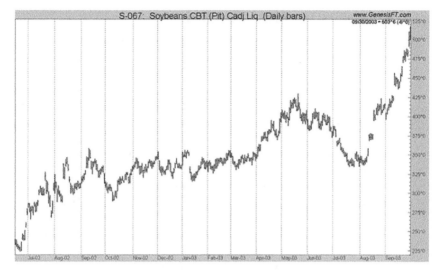

FIGURE 12.4 Soybeans Chart
Source: Genesis Financial Technologies, Inc. (www.GenesisFT.com).

If we can preframe ourselves and have a technique to follow, it will be easier to walk our talk through the fire and brimstone of actual trading.

If, and only if, you are in what you believe is a major uptrend or downtrend move, then you can use the lowest low of the last 17 days as your protective stop to exit the trade. If short, use the same thing in reverse, the highest high of the last 17 days. I exclude all inside days from the count and I'm talking trading days here, not calendar days. This will allow you to have plenty of leeway in your position, while still having a fail-safe point to exit the trend.

Once you are stopped out, you can reenter at the highest high of the last 13 days if it looks like the trend is again exerting itself. This simple rule will enable you to hold on for the ride—hopefully the ride of your life—to the point the market gets so wild that you exit at a target, simply because you have been in it 10 weeks or more. Few markets go up/down for more than 15 weeks without an important correction.

A GOOD WORD ON BAD HABITS

The truth is that more losses come from bad trading habits than from poor choices or bad systems. Here's a confession about my bad trading habits. I hope it helps you.

Bad Habits Are Worse Than Bad Advice

I'll take bad advice over bad habits any day of the week! Bad advice I can break away from, but habits, good or bad, are so ingrained in us that we stick with them. In this business sticking with what is bad is very bad.

For years my worst trading habit was plunging, trading too many contracts. I suspect this was due mostly to my impetuous youth—that burn to quickly prove yourself and make a killing. Plus, back then we really did not have even a concept of money management. That notion, that there are appropriate ways to marshal your hard-earned dollars, was not even discussed in the 1960s and 1970s.

Well, the long and short of it is that the habit of overtrading was pretty easy to break. I had no choice: it was break or be broken.

If this is your bad habit, let me plead with you to get off this path. It is perilous. It can punish you and even wipe you out. There is plenty of time to make money; don't rush or force this business. There is no time for losing money, and that is the ultimate product of overtrading.

The Habit of Getting a Habit

Habits are the product of success, and that's the problem. If you do something that works (that time) you will repeat that action to get the reward. If the same action works several times for you, you soon have a habit of acting or responding that way. The problem is that one swallow does not make a summer; the mere fact that some action was successful does not mean that on a long-term basis the optimum strategy is to repeat the action.

My worst trading habit, at this point, is to hold on to trades way too long. I looked at why I do that, and what I saw were several trades where I made substantial amounts of money and hence got reinforced to hold on. This began when, as a long-term trader, I made some real killings holding on through hell or high water. It is one of my strengths, but it's equally, I think, my largest weakness, especially as a short-term trader. What worked well for me in one time frame does not work well in another.

I assume if it is a weakness I have, most traders also have the same weakness. We are all pretty much alike.

I don't hold on to my losers. I'm willing to pitch them and use stops at all times. But the problem seems to be that once I get a winning trade on, I'll hold it past the obvious profit-taking point in hopes this will be the one big winner I want (need).

It boils down to this: high hopes for your winners in this business are dangerous. Don't let greed and those high hopes habitually cause you to hold on to positions past the obvious time or price profit-taking point.

CHAPTER 13

The One-Minute Commodity Trader

Instant gratification takes way too long.

It may seem like a bit of a stretch to say that you can spend one minute and know what to do in the markets. However, it's not too much of a stretch. What I want to share next is one of my favorite ways of using the commercial indicators. It begins with an idea, a concept that is important to understand. The concept is that we want to combine the trend of prices with the commercials' buying and selling.

If you have looked carefully at any of the charts presented so far you should have noticed that at times the commercials buy or sell too early, sometimes way too early. Yet the more you look the more you see that they often have an uncanny ability to buy and sell just before the start of major moves. Is there a way we can hone in on these exceptionally accurate junctures of buying and selling by our favorite players? I sure think there is, and to establish this point I want to take you step by step through this next lesson, first presenting a chart of what appears to be a somewhat erratic market vis-à-vis the commercials: bonds.

Figure 13.1 is the weekly chart, with the weekly percent of the six-month COT index. I have marked off each time the index dropped below 20 percent, suggesting a market top should be close at hand.

While some of these are very good, for example the one in late 1999 and the one in mid-2003, some of the other indications were too early. Some were good, some not so good, some bad. What seems to be needed is a little "cowboy luck." That's how many followers of the COT data have seen it over the years. Some of us have gone a step further to see if we

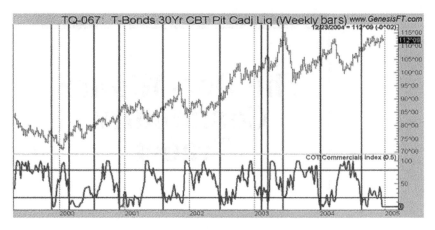

FIGURE 13.1 Treasury Bonds Chart
Source: Genesis Financial Technologies, Inc. (www.GenesisFT.com).

can't ferret out the good from the bad. This is not an easy job, but then if it was, everyone in the world would be doing this.

Wisdom in the art of speculation comes from looking and thinking. Here's an example, speaking of cowboys. If you see a pickup truck crossing dirt roads on the prairies with three guys in the cab wearing cowboy hats, how do you know which one is the real cowboy?

It's the one in the middle. Why? Well, he doesn't have to drive and he doesn't have to get out and open the gates. This is a simple answer, but unless you know cowboys and have tried to open a few tight fences, it's an answer you will never come up with. So it is with the markets. We have to look, to think, and then to keep our solutions as simple as possible.

Is there a solution to this—a one-minute solution? There sure is. In a moment I want to revisit this same chart with you. But first, let's talk a little about the marketplace, the trend of the markets, and a little more about the commercials.

TO MARKET, TO MARKET, TO CATCH A FAT PIG

Remember how I mentioned that the commercials are always in the marketplace, day in and day out? That's an important consideration. Since they are mining gold every day, cutting trees for lumber, or feeding cattle, they must, by the nature of their ongoing businesses, be constantly hedging their positions. This means that even in a down market that goes lower they will be buyers, or in an up market they will be sellers (on the hedge side). They are always there, buying and selling through their hedging operations.

They have to be there, while an astute speculator does not have to take action every day. Our advantage is that we can stay back in the shadows and pick a time and place to wage speculative war.

When you think about it, when should heavy commercial selling have the strongest impact on a market?

When the trend is up or the trend is down?

You got it, when the trend is down and the commercials become aggressive on the short side. In theory, we have the best of both worlds: a market that cannot rally, that has run into heavy selling pressures from the smartest guys in the business. With that in mind, let's look at the Treasury bond chart, looking to sell only when the trend is down.

Wait, though, how do we know if the trend is up or down? That is a good question and not an easy one to answer, even for me! Let's keep it really simple and say that as long as a 52-week moving average of price is higher than the prior week's, we are in an uptrend. The opposite is equally true; when the 52-week moving average is lower than it was one week ago we are in a downtrend. You can get fancier, use different trend measures and fancy mathematical formulas, but they all get pretty much to the same place—a general observation as to whether prices have been up or down.

With that in mind, please turn your attention to the same chart of bonds, with the 52-week moving average interlaced with price (Figure 13.2). More importantly, notice by this definition trend was down until

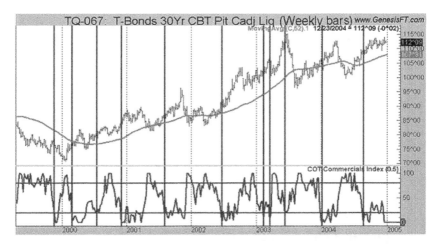

FIGURE 13.2 Treasury Bonds Chart
Source: Genesis Financial Technologies, Inc. (www.GenesisFT.com).

June 2000 (and was never again down), when the COT index entered the sell zone. What a filter! Sure, we missed the market slide starting in June 2003, but we sidestepped lots of premature selling indications from the commercials.

NOW ON THE BUY SIDE

The lesson is pretty simple: buy when trend is up and the COT index is in phase with the trend. In the bond example from 1999 through 2004, five and one-half years of action, we would have sidestepped all buy setups by the commercials until June 2000 and then taken buys only as the trend, the 52-week moving average, was up. Let's look at bonds now with that perspective and the buys marked off, and only the buys when the trend was up (see Figure 13.3).

My oh my, what do we have here? Winning buy setup after buy setup, and most of them coming just about on the button, not weeks or months early. In each instance the setups came with precious little risk. Suddenly, in less than a minute, we have been able to ferret out the best setups from the many!

Why this is so is based on an observation I made years ago and have come to respect regardless of the time frame one trades for:

The trend is the basis of all profits.

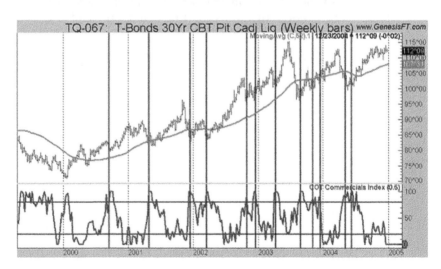

FIGURE 13.3 Treasury Bonds Chart
Source: Genesis Financial Technologies, Inc. (www.GenesisFT.com).

A man far wiser than I will ever be stated it a few centuries ago in yet another fashion:

An object once set in motion tends to stay in motion.

My understanding of these two corollaries is that we need to time a price movement to create market profits, and that once a trend gets rolling it's most likely to continue and is difficult to reverse, at least to quickly reverse, most of the time. I don't expect you to just take my notion of this or a chart or two as proof. So I'd like to present some more evidence of how effective this technique can be.

I ran a simple test of buying based on just two conditions. The first was that this week's 52-week moving average was greater than two weeks ago, and the second was that the six-month COT index was greater than 80 percent. That was it—nothing else, no more twists and turns. The results are shown in Table 13.1.

While I would never take down a position based on just this, indeed, it shows the bias of the setup, that when the commercials get bullish in an uptrend the best of the best opportunities appear.

Let's look at a few more examples to imprint the importance of this technique. Let's take the worst example I can think of, orange juice (Figure 13.4), the market that most COT followers say does not respond to the commercials' ins and outs.

In the time span from 2000 through 2004 there were only seven opportunities as defined by this trend filter. It would have been hard to have not made money with these setups. Granted, they don't take place often, but the method certainly gives us some wonderful opportunities.

As one more example, let's look at another market that has not, in recent years, been as responsive to just the COT report as many would like, wheat.

From 1998 through 2002 wheat (Figure 13.5) was in a strong downtrend (an object once set in motion) so all the COT buys were either short-lived or ineffective. Not so with the sells. Every time the commercials became heavy sellers, the rallies in wheat stalled, went sideways,

TABLE 13.1 Trading Results—Buying in an Uptrend

Commodity	Profit	Trades	Wins
British Pound	$51,311	21	71%
Bonds	$51,736	26	69%
Swiss Franc	$19,093	16	56%
S&P 500	$82,683	24	54%
Gold	$13,285	13	69%

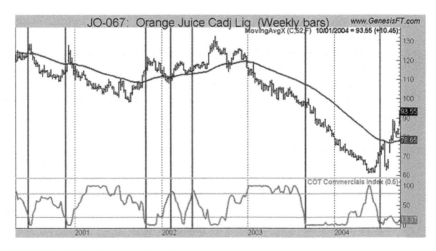

FIGURE 13.4   Orange Juice Chart
Source: Genesis Financial Technologies, Inc. (www.GenesisFT.com).

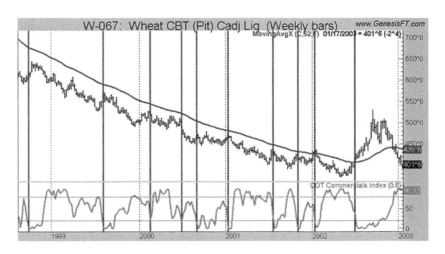

FIGURE 13.5   Wheat Chart
Source: Genesis Financial Technologies, Inc. (www.GenesisFT.com).

and then collapsed to new lows. It's no wonder. What we have here is a weak market in a classic and long-lived bear market. A trader's only question is when to get on the horse to ride. The answer is pretty simple, now that you have seen it and we have thought about it; when the commercials are heavy sellers in a downtrend new lows are most likely to follow.

Many Mansions . . .

There are several ways a speculator can trade off of this information. You may want to just take the trades as they come. Traders looking for larger percentage gains or those with a small amount of starting capital should consider these setups as the time to buy calls if in an uptrend, or puts when in a downtrend. These are the best option opportunities that I know of. We are combining powerful forces here, the all-pervasive trend with the adroit and informed commercials.

A ONE-MINUTE WONDER?

Once you get your charts set up it will certainly take less than one minute per week per chart to see if this setup exists. Usually it will not be there and you will flip to another chart. This pattern is not common. Just set up a moving average on your chart and the COT index. Then every weekend scan through the list of actively traded issues to find the nuggets of gold we are prospecting for.

Speaking of gold, I'd like you to turn your attention to the chart of gold in Figure 13.6 with the moving average and COT index. Keep in mind what you are looking for: COT selling in a downtrend puts us short, while COT buying in an uptrend tells us to become buyers.

Please take one—and only one—minute to see if you can't mark off

FIGURE 13.6 Gold Chart
Source: Genesis Financial Technologies, Inc. (www.GenesisFT.com).

the times you would have been a buyer or seller in that yellow metal that our economic world still revolves around.

That was not so difficult, was it? If the trend is down, take sells; sidestep them in an uptrend. Do we miss some great short selling points? You bet, we would have missed some profits. But we avoided a lot more questionable trades and several that would have taken money from us. As speculators we are always on the horns of a dilemma. One horn is to make as much money as we can, while the other is to not lose a single penny. It's kind of like having one foot forward, one ready to step back . . . we are at cross purposes. My sense of this is that it is wiser to focus more on not losing than on just winning. A loss can sap your energies, get you off mental focus, and can do a million other things to you, none of which are very good.

ALL YOU WANTED TO KNOW ABOUT GOLD

Without a doubt, more people follow the price of gold than any other commodity in the world, and with good reason. Gold, that archaic, barbaric precious metal men and women have coveted since the dawn of mankind, not only presents wonderful opportunities for making money, it also continues to have a major impact on currencies, interest rates, and markets across the globe.

While there are many factors that have some impact on this glittery metal, the ones that I have found to have the most impact are:

- The U.S. dollar relationship.
- The seasonal pattern.
- The commercials.
- Stock market crashes/depressions.

Gold and the Dollar

Let's start by looking at the relationship between gold and the dollar index, specifically the U.S. dollar. What seems to be going on is that gold can rally only so far above the U.S. dollar before it takes a tumble. It is difficult to see this relationship by looking at charts, but it is quite easy to see when you look at the spread relationship between these markets.

The relationship that I like to look at is arrived at by taking the spread between these two markets, on a weekly basis, then compiling a 3-week moving average of the spread and a 21-week moving average of the spread.

In order to see the "push-pull" of the spread, I then subtract the 3-week moving average from the 21-week moving average. Dividing that answer by 100 results in a uniform ratio; thus all points in time can be looked at on a consistent scale.

In doing this I have noticed that when this ratio gets out of whack—that is, the 3-week to the 21-week spread is greater than 30 percent—a market decline in gold will shortly exhibit itself. In other words, gold can get overbought versus the U.S. dollar, and at that point, large sums of professional money come in to take advantage of this imbalance by selling gold.

Figure 13.7 shows the tremendous impact this spread relationship has had over the past 15 years. Indeed, every time the spread has risen above the upper line you see here (30 percent), gold has tumbled.

Fundamental Lesson One: There is a relationship between the U.S. dollar and gold.

Figure 13.8 is an enlarged view of the late 1980s and early 1990s so you can get a better feel of the importance of this relationship or imbalance between gold and the U.S. dollar. This index can be followed or maintained weekly. You may also keep abreast of it, as I do, with the software from Genesis Financial Data Services (www.gfds.com).

Please note that this is not a day trading or short-term swing indicator. Its record is that of calling moves that last six months or longer. What I have developed, crude as it might be, is a way of discerning when gold is overvalued against the U.S. dollar. You may also see that most

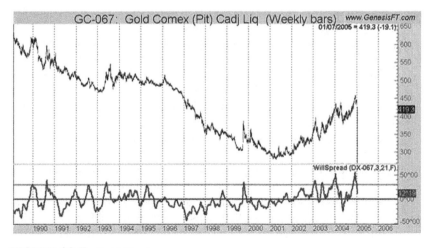

FIGURE 13.7 Gold Chart
Source: Genesis Financial Technologies, Inc. (www.GenesisFT.com).

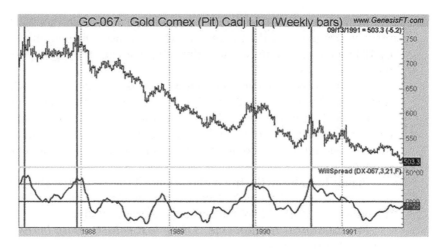

FIGURE 13.8 Gold Chart
Source: Genesis Financial Technologies, Inc. (www.GenesisFT.com).

major rallies in this metal, though not all, begin with this valuation index at a low level, suggesting that owning gold is better than owning dollars.

Does Gold Have a Seasonal Pattern?

We usually think of agricultural commodities like corn, cattle, and wheat or perhaps cocoa and coffee as having seasonal influences due to planting, harvesting, or breeding cycles. While that is true, it is equally true that the metal markets have shown a specific pattern to rally and decline, usually, but not always, at the same general time periods each year.

This is not a new idea. In my 1973 book, the first of its kind on identifying seasonal patterns in commodities (*How Seasonal Factors Influence Commodity Prices*, Windsor Books) I pointed out that gold had a seasonal influence to rally around July of each year with a top in December. As you look at the long-term price of gold in Figure 13.9, on a monthly chart, keep in mind that I wrote about the seasonal influence more than 30 years ago.

Underneath price you will see that the seasonal pattern (which has been exactly as I identified in 1973) rallies in the middle of the year and declines at the end. That's usually, not always, what gold does.

The chart in Figure 13.10 gives us a view of gold from 1993 into 2005, where we see the same general rule to be operative; that is, if gold is going to stage a good rally, the chances are high that it will come in the summer, while sells come at year-end.

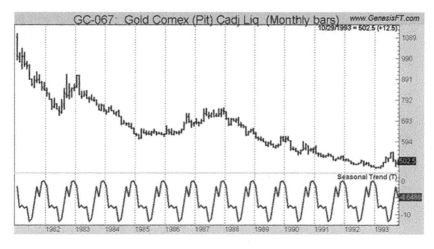

FIGURE 13.9 Gold Chart
Source: Genesis Financial Technologies, Inc. (www.GenesisFT.com).

This is important information. Virtually all of the sizable declines in gold came around the first of the year; this has not been a good time to be bullish on gold. It is a sucker play foisted upon the masses by the gold bug camp. The first of the year, when they make their gloom and doom prophecies of famine and pestilence, arguing for higher gold prices, is just not when it happens.

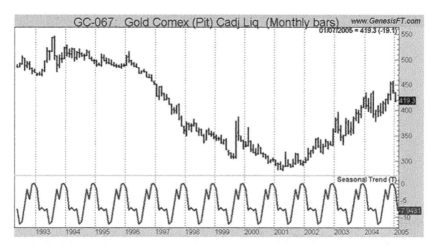

FIGURE 13.10 Gold Chart
Source: Genesis Financial Technologies, Inc. (www.GenesisFT.com).

Naturally, not every year is the same. There can and will be times when gold slips away from the seasonal influence. There is no perfection in this business of forecasting, but now you know the ideal times to look for rallies and declines in this market.

Fundamental Lesson Two: There is a time to sow and a time to reap gold—it has strong seasonal influences.

Watching the Commercials

There's no need for a channel changer as we watch the commercials in the gold market. The commercials I'm talking about here are a group of traders/investors called commercials by the U.S. government. These are the users and producers of commodities that are so large and influential that they must, by federal law, report all their buying and selling to the Commodity Futures Trading Commission every week.

These are the biggest, best, brightest, and deepest-pocket players of commodities in the world. They are the superpowers of finance and need to be followed like a hawk. I have been hawkeyeing this crowd since 1970 and would not take a position in any market without first seeing what they are doing. Now, I'll be the first to admit that there are still problems in using their track record of buying and selling to know what we should do. Yet, on balance, I do not know of any other tool with a better job of calling long-term market highs and lows.

Here, see for yourself a chart of gold in Figure 13.11 with my measure of commercial buying and selling underneath it.

As you can see, this chart stretches all the way back to the price of gold in 1984 and extends through 1990. In most instances when the index was high—meaning the commercials were heavy buyers—gold usually rallied, and when low, gold declined. Is it just that simple? Yes. Sure, there are nuances and subtleties to this, but by and large the commercials do the right thing most of the time. They are an excellent leading indicator of future price action.

Let's skip forward to 2002–2005 (Figure 13.12) and again look at the same index against the price of gold, and look what we see . . . déjà vu all over again. When the index is high, gold rallies, and when low, it gets spanked. Is it just that simple? Yes.

Fundamental Lesson Three: The future price of gold is heavily influenced by what the commercials do.

2 + 2 = 4 or How to Trade Gold   Look at what happened to gold in late 2004 (see Figure 13.12). The commercials have become heavy sellers

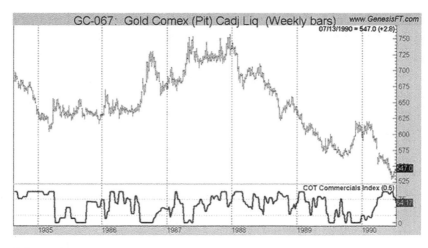

FIGURE 13.11 Gold Chart
Source: Genesis Financial Technologies, Inc. (www.GenesisFT.com).

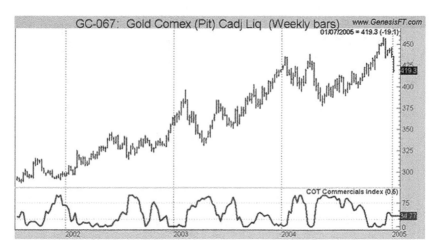

FIGURE 13.12 Gold Chart
Source: Genesis Financial Technologies, Inc. (www.GenesisFT.com).

and . . . and . . . did a bell just go off? I said, "late 2004." Isn't that the time when gold usually declines in phase with its seasonal pattern? Oh. "Gosh, I almost forgot. That sure enough is."

Depressions/Recessions and Stock Market Crashes

"Just wait until the market crashes and the economy goes to hell. Then gold will scream and the idiots will pay." I've heard that and similar verses to the point I'm angry. These people are the *idiots*. They have not studied the past. Gold did not have a rip-roaring bull market in 1929, or in the crash of 1970, or during the largest one-month decline in history in 1987. When markets around the world toppled in 2000 with the Nasdaq losing 75 percent in value, did gold soar to the moon?

Nope. Gold barely rallied.

I rest my case. Stock market crashes and depressions do not put gold higher. To that end, here is a chart of gold with a chart of the Dow 30 underneath it (Figure 13.13). Perhaps you can see what I can't. But for the life of me, I do not find any association with large rallies in the gold market and stock market declines. Go ahead. See for yourself.

Let's look past 1990 and see what happened in the crash of 2000—a crash heard around the world as economies went into a tailspin and unemployment approached 9 percent throughout Europe (see Figure 13.14).

While stocks plummeted, gold also declined and then had its best rally from about the start of 2002 to approximately mid-2002. At that same time

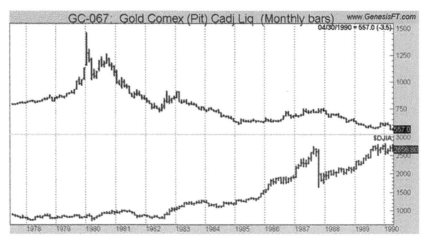

FIGURE 13.13 Gold Chart
Source: Genesis Financial Technologies, Inc. (www.GenesisFT.com).

FIGURE 13.14 Gold Chart
Source: Genesis Financial Technologies, Inc. (www.GenesisFT.com).

stocks were rallying! When stocks bottomed in early 2003, guess what? Gold bottomed and rallied in harmony with the stock market rally.

Point Counterpoint: Gold does not rally when stocks or economies collapse.

I can almost hear you now saying, "Okay, smart guy, when does gold rally based on market forces you have not mentioned earlier?"

My best answer is that when inflation goes berserk, expect gold to rally. The great gold bull market of 1979–1980 took place when Jimmy Carter, perhaps the worst president since Franklin Delano Roosevelt, was in power. Inflation and interest rates soared. Gold rallies when there is money around, and it is afraid of losing purchasing power. In depressions and recessions there is no money around to buy much of anything, anyway.

Once you learn to avoid losses all there is to worry about is winning!

There is no better way of avoiding losses than getting yourself in phase with the dominant trend. Trends persist, usually for far longer than we can ever imagine; so as long as the trend is one-sided, work that side of the market. Traders are a funny lot. We seem to like to argue. We'll even argue with the trend! Since it's human nature to want to buy low at what looks like a bottom, we will be buyers all the way down in a major bear market, arguing with the trend and trying to buy cheap. That's the way the human mind seems to be wired to work. We have to rewire our thought process to one of using the trend, of riding the trend and hopping aboard the trend when the commercials take a position in harmony with the existing trend.

All we really have to do is find a horse going in a known direction and saddle up. It's not any more complicated than that. But most of us, and that sure does include you, will fall into the trap of bottom picking, of thinking instead of responding to what is. We try to create what we think will be. It is so much easier to swim downstream; you get there faster, with less effort and toll on the body.

The trend remains our friend; the problem has been knowing how to use the trend. No longer, though, as you now have what I think is the best way of them all to use trend in our favor.

THOUGHTS IN A NEVER-ENDING BATTLE

I have enjoyed writing this book; such work forces one to rethink long-held ideas, to make them more concise and improve upon them. This book has been written as much for me as for you. The ultimate message I hope you have learned here is that the markets are not easy; they are full of risk . . . and equally full of reward.

The many years of trading have taught me two lessons: the markets are very simple and they are very complex. They are complex on a short-term basis, and simple on a longer-term basis. As a beginner, which I assume you are, it's really not much more complicated than to find a market where the commercials have heavy buyers relative to open interest, while the longer-term trend is up. Hopefully, you will also find a seasonal rally due about the same time and discover the public has been selling or refraining from buying.

That's very basic. It is all you need for a setup. There is not much need to look for more than this. See? It can be simple.

The next thing to do is look for an entry technique.

I've shown you a few here. You may have learned some from other authors or may have an idea or two of your own. Frankly, I'm not so certain mine are any better than yours or anyone else's; after all, regardless of the brilliance of our entry, the bottom line is we are just taking a shot and getting aboard a trend. Sure, some work better than others, but all can fail. That's why I have urged you to use stops. That's why I have counseled you not to plunge and overtrade.

The object is to hop aboard a move with protection from the get-go, our stop, and then use a trailing stop to ride the trend as we look for targets along the way. That's been my game plan, the plan that unfolded over the past 43 years of following markets, actually trading.

If you would like to see more of my work you may want to know that I give free updates on my web site at www.ireallytrade.com. Every week or so I do a mini-seminar on trading tools and tactics such as you have learned here. Thanks to the Internet I can show you a chart with the various indicators and you can hear me talk as I explain a lesson or describe what I see going on.

CHAPTER 14

Charts

What They Are, What They Mean

As scarce as truth is, the supply has always been in excess of the demand.

—Josh Billings

My suspicions are that most of my readers are well aware of the various forms of charting. Yet, I suppose many of you are not. So for you, here are the basic forms of charting for following the markets.

IT'S ALL ABOUT TIME

The art of being a successful trader is very much about time—the right time to take action and knowing what time frame you are trading for. The first lesson is:

The trend is the basis of all profits.

That is as true of a statement as you will ever read about the markets. Here is the second part of that idea.

Trends are a function of time.

By this I mean that the bigger a trend can be, the more time is needed. There is certainly a better shot at getting a large and profitable trend in 12 months than in 12 days, 12 hours, 12 minutes, or 12 seconds. In this business, time is our ally and we usually want more of it, not less, as it is the basis of all trends.

Now, the next thing you need to know is that time is different for everyone. Some people like to day trade, while others like to hold for a year or longer. You need to know what time frame works best for you.

For most beginners I think the ideal time frame is a week to three months if we can spot such major moves. These are the definitions of time that I use:

- Long term—A year or more.
- Intermediate term—Three months to 11 months.
- Short term—Two to 60 days.
- Day trade—In today, out today, a matter of hours.

PROS AND CONS OF CHARTS

Market followers need something to go by, so we have turned to a wide variety of ways to watch the action. Usually we watch charts, which are records, or pictures if you will, of what price action has looked like. Chart watchers can see quite a bit. We can see the trend over various time periods. We can see prior times of support and resistance in hopes of being better speculators in the future. I can't imagine taking a position in the market without looking at the price action; perhaps I'm just a more visual person, but I think most are like me.

To that end, humankind has come up with many ways of looking at price activity. I'd like to show you the major ones in this chapter and will add my comments as I see fit. My most important comment is that chart watchers are called technicians or technical analysts, as they/we try to figure out the future based just on the chicken scratches of price action rather than the fundamentals of the marketplace. Let me jump right in here and tell you that I do not have a lot of agreement with the technical guys and gals. Sure, I think there is a place for looking at charts. They can show quite a bit, but they are a reflection of the past, and the past, despite what you might think, has difficulty in predicting the future. I like to look at charts for the following purposes:

- To determine the trend.
- To look for emotional binges.
- To find patterns that I know act as springboards to moves.
- To find places where breakouts or breakdowns can be used for entries or stops.

I am not of the school that charts "know all and show all," nor do I think that "there is no greater indication of what the market is doing than the market itself." I think charts are overused. Why? Well, they short-circuit the logical process. One glance at a chart and you think you know or have learned something. Real knowledge comes from studying the conditions that cause the markets to move, as I have repeatedly discussed herein. There are other factors, particularly for stocks; see my book *The Right Stock at the Right Time* (Wiley, 2003).

With this in mind, let's take a look at the various ways of looking at price action.

OPEN, HIGH, LOW, AND CLOSE CHARTS

Figure 14.1 is an example of the most widely used chart in the world, the open, high, low, and close chart. Each day the market follower or chartist records where prices opened (the horizontal line on the left of the bar), the daily high, and the daily low, and then makes a line on the right of the bar where prices closed that day, or week, or whatever time frame one is monitoring. This daily bar chart is the type of chart I use. I prefer these charts, I suppose in part because these are what I cut my speculative teeth on, and they have been around longer than most of the other forms you are going to see.

What's important about a chart is that it helps you see what has been going on in the marketplace, and may in some fashion capture the sentiment of what traders have been doing and indicate the trend of prices. I

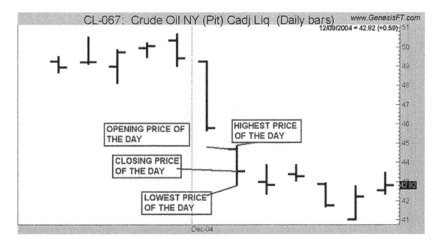

FIGURE 14.1 Crude Oil Open, High, Low, and Close Chart
Source: Genesis Financial Technologies, Inc. (www.GenesisFT.com).

think daily bars do this quite well. Admittedly, the candlestick charts that you will see next have become very popular and also provide the same information. The candlestick crowd makes all sorts of claims to the effect that they allow one to see what is not there at first glance. I have not been able to prove that, despite some heated arguments and presentations of data. Until it's been proven otherwise, you will find me gazing at bar charts.

CANDLESTICK CHARTS

Supposedly developed in Japan hundreds of years ago, candlestick charts have become a fashionable way of following the markets. Try as I might, I have not been able to duplicate the claims of promoters of this technique. Here's how it works. Japanese candlesticks supposedly offer a glimmer into the psychology of short-term trading activity. Candlesticks can show whether the buyer or seller has control of the market. The high and low of the day are described as shadows and plotted as a single line.

The price range between the open and close is plotted as a rectangle on the single line. If the close is above the open, the body of the rectangle is white. If the close is below the open, the body of the rectangle is black. So an up close makes for a white bar, a down close for a black one. Followers of these formations have many claims, but they have not been substantiated by computer studies. They are, I suspect, very much an art form.

Figure 14.2 is a typical chart showing this technique.

FIGURE 14.2   Crude Oil Candlestick Chart
Source: Genesis Financial Technologies, Inc. (www.GenesisFT.com).

Lighting Fires

A paper seemingly validating this form of charting by Gunduz Caginalp and Henry Laurent, "The Predictive Power of Price Patterns," from the University of Pittsburgh Mathematics Department (www.pitt.edu/~caginalp /Paper65.pdf), got the candlestick crowd all lit up.

The abstract report makes a very bold claim: that these patterns produced gains of 1 percent over a two-day hold. That is a phenomenal rate of return, one that got me to open my computer up to see if I could make 1 percent every other day with these patterns. Here's what the abstract said:

> *Using two sets of data, including daily prices (open, close, high, and low) of all S&P 500 stocks between 1992 and 1996, we perform a statistical test of predictive capability of candlestick patterns. Out-of-sample tests indicate statistical significance at the level of 36 standard deviations from the null hypothesis, and indicate a profit of almost 1 percent during a two-day holding period. An essentially nonparametric test utilizes standard definitions of three-day candlestick patterns and removes conditions on magnitudes. The results provide evidence that traders are influenced by price behavior. To the best of our knowledge, this is the first scientific test to provide strong evidence in favor of any trading rule or pattern on a large unrestricted scale.*

When I tried to duplicate the study's results, I was not able to come anywhere close to these numbers. I ran it on just the S&P 500 futures (many reasons why I prefer that) so that is the only thing not like theirs, but I think the S&P 500 is a better test than individual stocks. Also, I'm not the brightest candle on the cake, but my first volley confirms what many prior tests show: candlestick charts are not something that one can easily make into a mechanical system of trading.

A fellow trader e-mailed in response to my comments on this report, "While I have not attempted to reproduce the article's programming, I can say that I have programmed several candlestick patterns as entries, using fixed exits, and they do not, in general, perform even marginally acceptably on futures contracts, be it S&P or others."

I programmed several of the best buy patterns in the candlestick books and could not get any of them to work nearly as well as advertised. That's why my view is that although they may be very helpful in letting a trader see what has been going on, so far I have not been able to make a successful trading pattern with them. This view is unchanged from the article I wrote regarding this form of charting for *Futures* magazine more than 10 years ago. To my way of thinking, candlesticks have not met the test of time.

CLOSING-ONLY PRICE CHARTS

The next chart shows records of only the closing prices of the stock or commodity. The open, high, and low are not used; one merely records each day's close and tries to determine the trend from there. This is a simple way of following markets, but it leaves a lot of information out. In a market that does not have wild swings such a presentation of the data works quite well. The rub is that price may close at 60 today and close at 85 tomorrow. Since we cannot take action until the close at 85 we missed 25 points of intraday market movement. That's too much for me to miss. Figure 14.3 is such a chart.

MARKET PROFILE CHARTS

Market Profile in commodity futures is a trademark of the Chicago Board of Trade (CBOT) (1984) that refers to a specific data structure derived from the CBOT Liquidity Data Bank (LDB). A Market Profile is a price-time display of cleared price at time and a value calculated from cleared volume at price. First published in 1985 and updated in 1991, in the CBOT Market Profile manual the term "Market Profile" has become, over time, a somewhat generic name to describe auction market analyses on a variety of markets outside of CBOT (e.g., *Steidlmayer on Markets*, 2nd ed., Wiley, 2002, pp. 84, 93). J. Peter Steidlmayer is the developer of the technique.

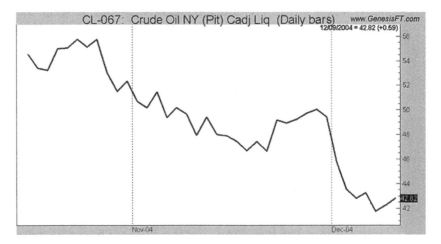

FIGURE 14.3 Crude Oil Closing-Only Chart
Source: Genesis Financial Technologies, Inc. (www.GenesisFT.com).

Market Profile people make funny-looking (to me, not them) charts where they break down each 30 minutes of trading activity into horizontal bars as in Figure 14.4.

The price/time profile is completely dynamic, and displays a horizontally positioned histogram that graphs a time-price relationship for trade in a security. Each half hour of the day is designated by a letter. If a certain price is traded during a given half hour, the corresponding letter is marked next to the price. The first half hour (or portion thereof) of trade will be noted with the letter *A*, the second half hour will be noted with the letter *B*, and so on. The open price for the day is marked with the letter *O*. As price moves up and down, each letter is marked only once at each price level.

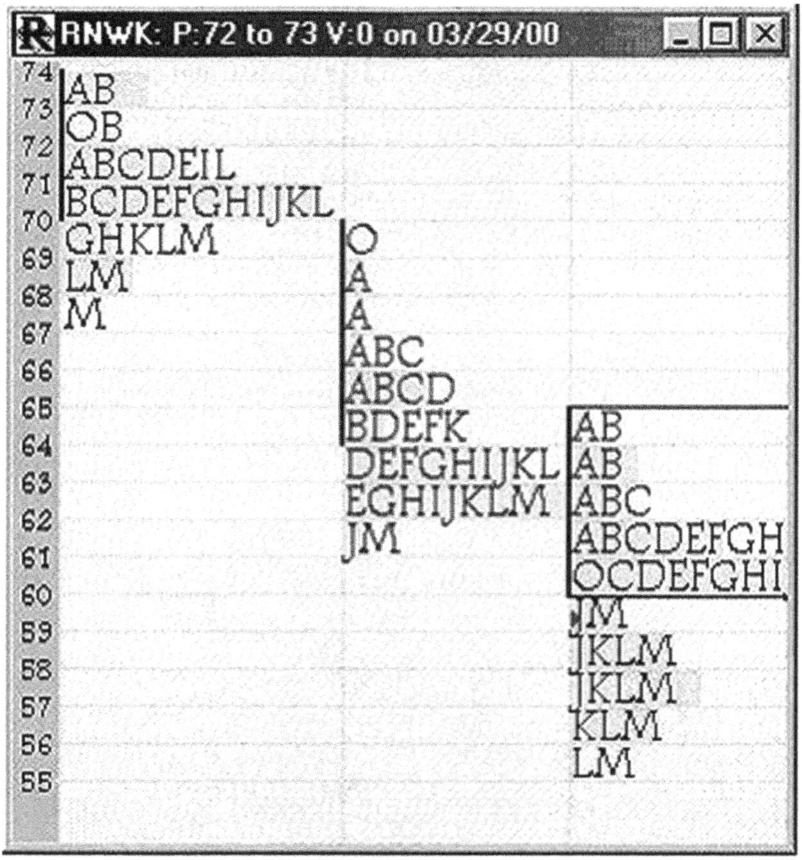

```
RNWK: P:72 to 73 V:0 on 03/29/00        _ □ ×

74 AB
73 OB
72 ABCDEIL
71 BCDEFGHIJKL
70 GHKLM        O
69 LM           A
68 LM           A
67 M            A
66              ABC
65              ABCD
64              BDEFK      AB
63              DEFGHIJKL   AB
62              EGHIJKLM   ABC
61              JM         ABCDEFGH
60                         OCDEFGHI
59                         JM
58                         JKLM
57                         JKLM
56                         KLM
55                         LM
```

FIGURE 14.4 Horizontal Bar Chart (Market Profile)

I have several friends who swear by these charts, and a few that swear at them like we do at all charts. The advocates of Market Profile charts think this form of charting allows them to see where support and resistance are in the marketplace. Thus the charts may have their greatest value for stops and entries in very short-term time frames. I did spend a month or so plotting these by hand in 1986 but could not make much of them . . . and that may tell you more about me than the chart.

POINT-AND-FIGURE CHARTS

This was once a very popular way of following stocks and commodities. It seems to have fewer followers now than in years past. It does not use time, which seems to be its claim to fame, and is not concerned about price changes smaller than a certain amount. Point-and-figure charts, so called I think because after having a losing trade you point at the chart and try to figure out what you did wrong, are kind of like vertical Market Profile charts.

As shown in Figure 14.5, a point-and-figure chart has price on the y-axis and time on the x-axis, but the time function is not regular because prices are plotted on the chart only when they represent significant movements. To plot a point-and-figure chart, therefore, you first need to decide what a significant amount of price change is. Whenever a price rise of that increment occurs, you mark the chart with an *X*, and you continue mark-

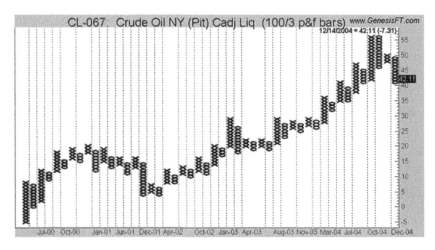

FIGURE 14.5 Crude Oil Point-and-Figure Chart
Source: Genesis Financial Technologies, Inc. (www.GenesisFT.com).

ing it vertically as long as the changes are heading in the same direction (i.e., up). When they change direction and start heading down, you start a new line (going over one column or box) on the x-axis and mark the chart with an *O*.

In 1968 I traded with a medical doctor who used these charts. He told me he liked them because "I can follow 200 stocks a day, they are so easy to keep up." I never saw it that way. I want to follow as few stocks as possible to be focused on what I do. I have found precious little use for this form of charting. I have no respect for it in any manner. Blunt enough? Yes, and it will get me in trouble with the true believers, but frankly, folks, I don't put that much stock in charts and technical analysis.

You know why: the commercials move the markets, not some special form of charting. Charts show us where a market has been, while the COT data tell us where it is most likely to go—and that's what I'm most interested in.

The idea behind point-and-figure charts is that by ignoring trivial price fluctuations, the overall trend is made much clearer. What you see on the chart is a clear pattern of significant price movements up and down.

KAGI BARS

These are like point-and-figure charts in that time is not a consideration, only boxes are not used. First you will need to choose a reversal amount—say 3 percent. This is called the "base price." If the closing price of Day 2 is greater than the closing price of Day 1 (the base price), draw a thick vertical line upward from the closing price of Day 1 to the closing price of Day 2. (See Figure 14.6.)

If the closing price of Day 2 is less than the closing price of Day 1, draw a thin vertical line downward from the closing price of Day 1 to the closing price of Day 2. If the closing price of Day 2 is equal to the closing price of Day 1, do nothing. Instead, wait until the end of Day 3, and compare this price with the base price. If the closing price continues to rise (or fall), we keep moving the kagi chart up (or down) to the close of each day, regardless of how much or how little it moves.

If the closing price moves in the opposite direction by less than a predetermined percentage, the reversal amount, we ignore the small move and do nothing to our chart. If the kagi line has been moving upward, and the closing price has fallen by more than the reversal amount, we draw a short horizontal line, called the "inflection line," then a new line downward, to the lower close of that day.

If the kagi line has been moving downward and the closing price has

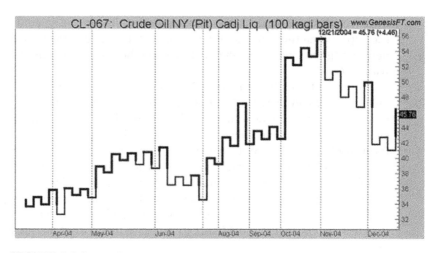

FIGURE 14.6 Crude Oil Kagi Bar Chart
Source: Genesis Financial Technologies, Inc. (www.GenesisFT.com).

risen by more than the reversal amount, we draw an inflection line, then a new line upward, to the higher close of that day.

RENKO CHARTS

The name of this type of chart stems from the Japanese word for bricks, *renga*. Like point-and-figure and kagi, it also does not look at time as a factor. In a renko chart, a line (or "brick" as they're called) is drawn in the direction of the prior move only if prices move by a minimum amount (i.e., the box size). The bricks are always equal in size. For example, in a five-unit renko chart, a 20-point rally is displayed as four five-unit-tall renko bricks. (See Figure 14.7.)

Basic trend reversals are signaled with the emergence of a new white or black brick. A new white brick indicates the beginning of a new uptrend. A new black brick indicates the beginning of a new downtrend. Since the renko chart is a trend-following technique, there are many times when renko charts produce whipsaws, giving signals near the end of short-lived trends. However, the hope of a trend-following technique is that it will allow you to ride the big uptrends and downtrends.

Since a renko chart isolates the underlying price trend by filtering out the minor price changes, renko charts are supposed to be helpful when determining support and resistance levels.

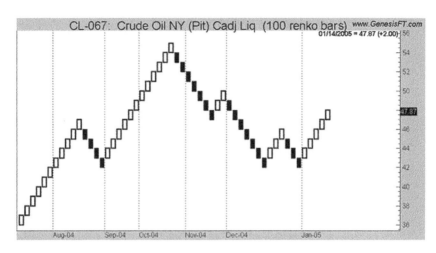

FIGURE 14.7 Crude Oil Renko Chart
Source: Genesis Financial Technologies, Inc. (www.GenesisFT.com).

MORE CHART JARGON: MOVING AVERAGES

Moving averages are one of the oldest and most popular technical analysis tools. They have been with us since speculation began.

A moving average is the average price of a stock or commodity for a given time period. When calculating a moving average, you specify the time span to calculate the average price (e.g., 18 days).

A simple moving average is calculated by adding prices for the most recent n time periods and then dividing by n—for example, adding the closing prices of gold for the most recent 18 days and then dividing by 18. The result is the average price over the past 18 days. This calculation is done for each period in the chart.

Note that a moving average cannot be calculated until you have n time periods of data. For example, you cannot display an 18-day moving average until the 19th day in a chart. The next chart, Figure 14.8, shows an 18-day simple moving average of the closing price of gold.

Since the moving average in this chart is the average price over the last 18 days, it represents the trend of investor expectations over that time. If the price is above its moving average, it means that investors' current expectations (i.e., the current price) are higher than their average expectations over the last 18 days, and that investors are becoming increasingly bullish on the security. Conversely, if today's price is below its moving average, this shows that current expectations are below average expectations over the last 18 days.

FIGURE 14.8 Gold Chart with Simple Moving Average
Source: Genesis Financial Technologies, Inc. (www.GenesisFT.com).

The classic interpretation of a moving average is to use it to observe changes in prices. Investors typically buy when the price rises above its moving average and sell when the price falls below its moving average.

Is that a good approach? No, it is not. I know this as a fact from testing various moving averages and various versions of what a valid crossover is. On their own none of them consistently make money. That does not mean that they cannot be used as a tool. One example would be to buy when the price crosses above a moving average by a certain threshold at the same time that the commercials have been heavy buyers. Figure 14.9 shows, with lines, all the crossovers and illustrates just how much, on its own, a moving average can be whipsawed.

The moving average club has tried a plethora of tricks to make this stuff work, such as using two, three, or four moving averages. One fellow's chart I saw had 30 different averages. Give me a break. *What doesn't work can't be made to work by having more of the same.* Others will hand select examples of a moving average that works perfectly for the chart they show you, but does not work at any other times. I can do that, too. Figure 14.10 is again of gold and with an 18-day moving average but for a different time period. Gee, this looks like the surefire way to wealth until you know I hand selected it, as most authors, system sellers, and lecturers are prone to do.

I do like and will use these averages to help me identify the trend so I can get in phase with the underlying slope of the market. In the gold

FIGURE 14.9 Gold Chart with Crossovers
Source: Genesis Financial Technologies, Inc. (www.GenesisFT.com).

chart shown, as a short-term trader I would have worked the long side of this market whenever the moving average was trending up, the short side when it was trending down. If I see the trend is up and the commercials have been buying, that's an ideal setup. On its own I shy away from this tool; only in conjunction with other tools have I found it to be of value.

FIGURE 14.10 Hand Selected Gold Chart
Source: Genesis Financial Technologies, Inc. (www.GenesisFT.com).

DON'T PUT YOUR CHARTS BEFORE THE HORSE

I like to be in phase with the trend. Swimming upstream is hard work. Have you ever tried it? I still recall the first time I went skinny-dipping in the "Big Ditch" in my home town of Billings, Montana, on a moonlit night and tried to swim against the current to get back to where my clothes were squirreled away at a hiding spot we called Plymouth Rock. Man, it was almost impossible. I only had to swim about 20 feet, and the ditch doesn't flow that fast. Yet it took all the energy I could muster, and I was a competitive swimmer. Looking back on it, I guess that was my first lesson in speculation, a message I have not always listened to and have failed to heed usually at my expense.

Another way of looking at this is the difference between running uphill and downhill. Even a slight 2 percent increase in grade makes for a much slower marathon. There is no magic to the number of days in a moving average; the magic is in getting into alignment with the trend. The problem is that traders like to argue, like to defy the trend; they think the big money is made in buying absolute market bottoms. Indeed that is a correct thought. The problem is that it is almost impossible to attain that goal.

I can think of two or three other ways of representing price actions on chart views not discussed here or used, that I know of, by anyone else. I'm sure there's a good deal of money to be made by introducing some new form of charting. Every few years someone cooks up a new chart book. I'd rather make my money from trading charts, not selling them. How is that done?

Hopping aboard a trend is the secret to chart reading. Go with the flow if you want to make serious dough.

CHART PATTERNS AND SUCH

Once you master the various forms of charts, something I have not been able to do, the next maze to wander through consists of the various patterns chartists claim have predictive power. You will hear of wedges, pennants, flags, triangles, heads and shoulders, boxes, Ws and Ms, and all sorts of chart-speak that I have never been able to make much sense of. It becomes a subject unto itself. One type of wedge on a chart, a rising wedge, has been defined as a bearish pattern that begins wide at the bottom and contracts as prices move higher and the trading range narrows. In contrast to symmetrical triangles, which have no definitive slope and no bullish or bearish bias, rising wedges definitely slope up and have a bearish bias. The best book on the subject, *Encyclopedia of Chart Patterns*, by Thomas Bulkowski (Wiley, 2000), lists 11 different patterns a wedge can take.

The most common chart patterns you will hear about, and see, are shown in Figure 14.11. Perhaps against the backdrop of what the superpowers are doing they take on more meaning.

As I see it, these patterns are more a function of charting than some hidden code to market action. Chart patterns do not need a magic decoder ring to become oracles of our future. You can chart any—yes, any—set of data and get the same patterns the chart guys write dissertations about, so what's real? If the same chart pattern can be depicted in pork bellies and also seen on a chart of temperature ranges on Chicago, are we dealing with anything of merit?

SUPPORT AND RESISTANCE

Well, I've drawn the line across the chart room floor, so I might as well bring on the full wrath of chartists around the world. These poor deluded folks think that markets find support and resistance at certain places on their charts. There are many supposed systems for identifying where a market will turn based on price or time ratios. I don't have the time, space, or inclination to demolish all of them, so I will just attack the most popular—the arcane notion that markets move according to something called Fibonacci ratios.

THE FIB OF FIBONACCI

Like all newcomers to this game, I heard of the ratios and began using them just like the books said. I lost money. I tried other ratios and refinements of Fibonacci. I lost more money. The advocates assured me this approach worked. I talked to other "Fib" traders and found we had something in common; they were losing just like me. Let's look at the ratio and its history.

The ratio Leonardo Fibonacci devised was the product of his investigation of the rate at which rabbits multiply. Rabbits and stocks, that makes sense! The ratio is expressed in a sequence of numbers in which each number is the sum of the two preceding numbers. Thus: 1, 1, 2, 3, 5, 8, 13, 21, 34, 55, and so on.

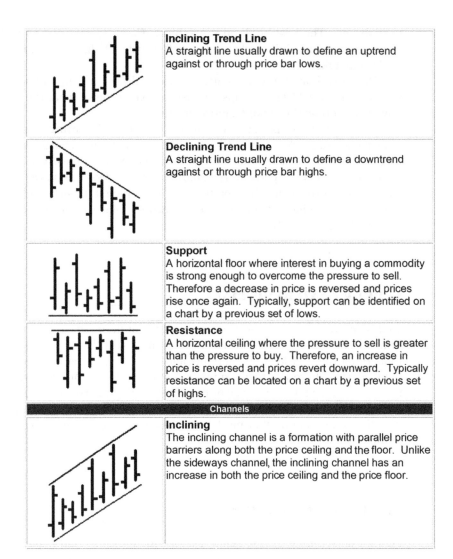

| **Inclining Trend Line** A straight line usually drawn to define an uptrend against or through price bar lows. |
| **Declining Trend Line** A straight line usually drawn to define a downtrend against or through price bar highs. |
| **Support** A horizontal floor where interest in buying a commodity is strong enough to overcome the pressure to sell. Therefore a decrease in price is reversed and prices rise once again. Typically, support can be identified on a chart by a previous set of lows. |
| **Resistance** A horizontal ceiling where the pressure to sell is greater than the pressure to buy. Therefore, an increase in price is reversed and prices revert downward. Typically resistance can be located on a chart by a previous set of highs. |

Channels

| **Inclining** The inclining channel is a formation with parallel price barriers along both the price ceiling and the floor. Unlike the sideways channel, the inclining channel has an increase in both the price ceiling and the price floor. |

FIGURE 14.11   Chart Patterns

These examples were taken from Gecko Software's *Track 'n Trade Pro Software Manual.* I thank Gecko Software for allowing reproduction rights (www.Track nTrade.com).

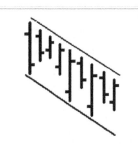

Declining
The declining channel is a formation with parallel price barriers along both the price ceiling and the floor. Unlike the sideways channel, the declining channel has a decrease in both the price ceiling and the price floor.

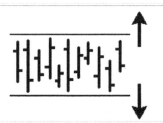

Horizontal or Sideways
A horizontal or sideways channel is a formation that features both resistance and support. Support forms the low price barrier, while resistance provides the price ceiling.

Triangles

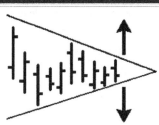

Symmetrical
A formation in which the slopes of price highs and lows are converging to a point so as to outline the pattern in a symmetrical triangle. To trade this formation, place a buy order on a break up and out of the triangle or a sell order on a break down and out of the triangle.

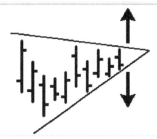

Nonsymmetrical
A formation in which the slopes of price highs and lows are converging to a point so as to outline the pattern in a nonsymmetrical triangle. To trade this formation, place a buy order on a break up and out of the triangle or a sell order on a break down and out of the triangle.

(Continues)

FIGURE 14.11 *(Continued)*

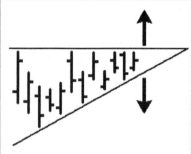

Ascending

A formation in which the slopes of price highs and lows come together at a point outlining the pattern of a right triangle. The hypotenuse in an ascending triangle should be sloping upward from left to right. To trade this formation, place a buy order on a break up and out of the triangle or a sell order on a break down and out of the triangle. Ascending triangles with a prior downtrend are anticipated to break down and out, rather than up and out.

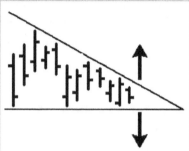

Descending

A formation in which the slopes of price highs and lows come together at a point outlining the pattern of a right triangle. The hypotenuse in a descending triangle should be sloping downward from left to right. To trade this formation, place a buy order on a break up and out of the triangle or a sell order on a break down and out of the triangle. Descending triangles with a prior uptrend are anticipated to break up and out, rather than down and out.

Pennants

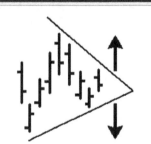

Pennants

A formation in which the slopes of price bar highs and lows are converging to a point so as to outline a pattern similar to a symmetrical triangle but generally stubbier or not as elongated. To trade this formation, you can place orders at both the break up and out of the pennant and break down and out of the pennant.

FIGURE 14.11   *(Continued)*

Wedges

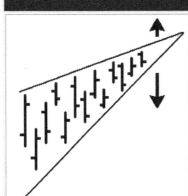

Rising or Inclining

This formation occurs when the slopes of price bar highs and lows join at a point forming an inclining wedge. The slopes of both lines are up with the lower line being steeper than the higher one. To trade this formation, place an order on a break up and out of the wedge or a sell order on a break down and out the wedge. Rising wedges with a prior downtrend are anticipated to break down and out, rather than up and out.

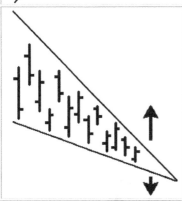

Falling or Declining

This formation occurs when the slopes of price bar highs and lows join at a point forming a declining wedge. The slopes of both lines are down with the upper line being steeper than the lower one. To trade this formation, place an order on a break up and out of the wedge or a sell order on a break down and out the wedge. Falling wedges with a prior uptrend are anticipated to break up and out, rather than down and out.

Flags

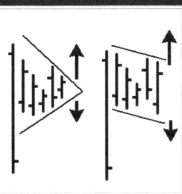

Bull Flag

A formation consisting of a small number of price bars where the slopes of price bar highs and lows are parallel and declining. Bull flags are identified by their characteristic pattern and by the context of the prior trend. In the case of a bull flag the trend leading to its formation is up. To trade this formation, place orders on the break up and break down points, leaving your unfilled order as your stop loss.

(Continues)

FIGURE 14.11 *(Continued)*

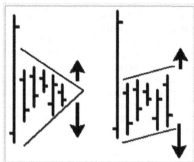

Bear Flag

A formation consisting of a small number of price bars in which the slopes of price bar highs and lows are parallel and inclining. Bear flags are identified by their characteristic pattern and by the context of the prior trend. In the case of a bear flag the trend leading to its formation is down. To trade this formation, place buy and sell orders on the break up and down of the flag, leaving the unfilled order as your stop loss.

Top and Bottom Formations

1-2-3 (A-B-C) Top

Anticipates a change in trend from up to down on a break below the number 2 point.

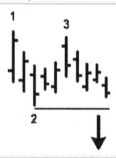

1-2-3 (A-B-C) Bottom

Anticipates a change in trend from down to up on a break above the number 2 point.

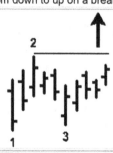

FIGURE 14.11 *(Continued)*

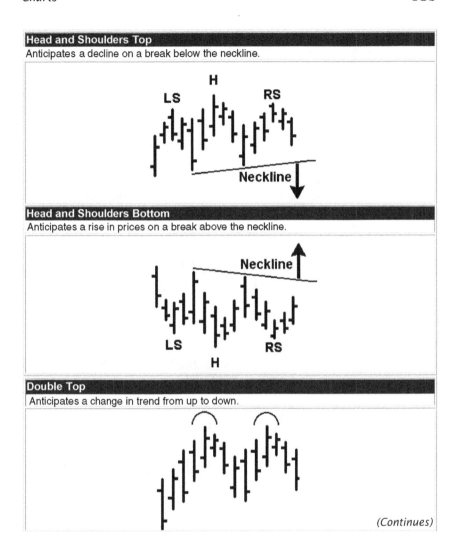

Head and Shoulders Top

Anticipates a decline on a break below the neckline.

Head and Shoulders Bottom

Anticipates a rise in prices on a break above the neckline.

Double Top

Anticipates a change in trend from up to down.

(Continues)

FIGURE 14.11 *(Continued)*

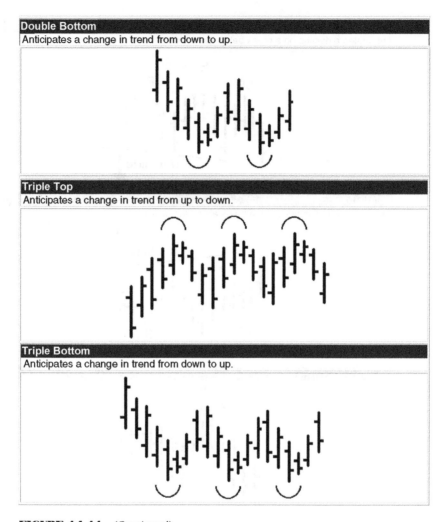

FIGURE 14.11 *(Continued)*

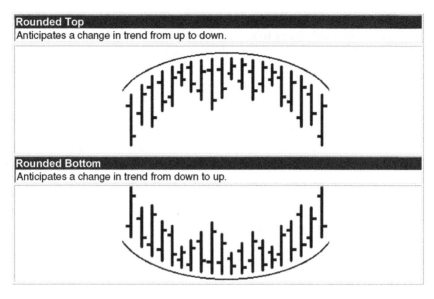

Rounded Top
Anticipates a change in trend from up to down.

Rounded Bottom
Anticipates a change in trend from down to up.

FIGURE 14.11 *(Continued)*

This sequence discovered by Fibonacci, an Italian mathematician who lived from 1170 to 1250, has, admittedly, proved useful in many different areas of mathematics and science. I had the great pleasure of walking on Fibonacci Boulevard in Pisa, Italy, with my partner Louise Stapleton a few years ago. All I could think of was what would he think of stock folks using his ratios?

What Is the Ratio Traders Speak Of?

Fibonacci numbers are interconnected with several ratios, the most common being:

$$1/1 = 1$$
$$2/1 = 2$$
$$3/2 = 1.5$$
$$5/3 = 1.6666\ldots$$
$$8/5 = 1.6$$
$$13/8 = 1.625$$
$$21/13 = 1.6153\ldots$$
$$34/21 = 1.6190\ldots$$

If you keep on going for a long time, the ratios settle down. They all get closer and closer to a number without ever quite reaching it. There's a name for this phenomenon when it happens in math—it's called a "limit." You can say that the limiting ratio of Fibonacci numbers as the numbers get higher and higher is the definition of the Golden Ratio. It's not exactly 8/5, but it's close. The exact value of the Golden Ratio is $(1 + 5^{1/2})/2$, which is about 1.6180339.

I don't know if you've studied algebra or if you know about quadratic equations and the tricks people use for solving them. In case these things are familiar and interesting to you, here's a fact you might investigate:

The ratios of Fibonacci numbers get closer and closer to the Golden Ratio, but they never quite get there. You can prove that if they *did* ever get there, then they wouldn't change anymore, but would stay equal to the Golden Ratio forever after that.

The key ratio is that these numbers are always 1.6 (or close to it) of the prior number: 1.6 times 5 = 8. There is also a 0.38 relationship in that 0.38 of, say, 13 is 5. Subtract 5 from 13 and you have 8. Chartists see these numbers as retracements and will tell you markets also retrace on this same format. The Fibonacci number sequence is created by adding the last two numbers in the sequence to create the next number (1, 1, 2, 3, 5, 8, 13, 21, 34, 55). The first three numbers in the sequence are normally dropped for analysis purposes. The number sequence creates some interesting mathematical relationships. The most commonly used are: the ratio of any number to its next higher number that approaches a constant value of 0.618 (e.g., 34/55 = 0.618, 55/89 = 0.618); the ratios of alternate numbers that approach a constant 0.382 (e.g., 21/55 = 0.382, 34/89 = 0.382). For those who are mathematically inclined, 0.382 is also the inverse of 0.618 (i.e., 1 – 0.618 = 0.382).

Chart watchers use Fibonacci ratios by drawing horizontal lines using the ratios 0.618, 0.50, and 0.382 measured from high or low points. These lines are often useful in identifying retracement points where you might look to be a buyer/seller. Let's say prices have rallied from 35 to 90 for a total distance traveled of 55 points. Fib believers will look for the market to retrace in units of 0.38 of that amount down to 68.9, 0.50 of that amount to 62.5, or a 0.62 retracement back to 55.9.

Got it? A market runs up and then we can buy on a pullback to these levels. Of course if a level is broken, then the retracement goes—or should go—to the next level.

A quick check on the Internet will reveal ads for this approach. Some are glitzed up a bit from this, but they are all based on what I have explained. The ads will say things like "Magic Method," "Predict the Markets and Win," or "Trading Made Easy," with all sorts of claims about how great these numbers are and how easy trading with them can be.

Don't get suckered in here. . . . 'Tain't that way. Here's a report I wrote a few years back. I'm bound to stir up a hornets' nest with this, but the truth has got to come out, I'm here to tell you.

Fibonacci Retracements Are at Best a Bad Tool, at Worst a Hoax

I have many friends who use Fibonacci levels; some have written books about it, while others have made careers over these numbers. They are nice people. Yet what I'm about to show you is harsh evidence that there is no significance to these supposed support points.

The ratio of these numbers has had market guys all abuzz since the early 1900s, so I've got a large task here to repeal over 100 years of a belief system. But that's just what I'm going to do, right here in front of your eyes.

Followers of Fibonacci stake their main work on the ratio of 0.618 (or rounded off 0.62). Each number in any Fibonacci sequence is approximately 1.62 times the previous number and about 0.62 times the next number. If we divide 21 by 34 we get approximately 0.62. Divide 34 by 21 and we have, drumroll here, 1.62.

Step back a moment and divide 8 by 21, one step back, and we have 0.38, the next big Fib number.

How They Say It Works

This camp of true believers has written, time and time again, that when markets rally the ensuing pullbacks (declines) will stop at a percent retracement of the up move. If price rallied from 30 to 80, a rally of 50 points, the pullback from this rally should (they say "must" or "will") come at amounts equal to 38 percent of 50, 50 percent of 50, or 62 percent of 50. Should the decline take out the low at 30, it should stop at 1.38 percent or 1.62 percent of 50. I think this is a fair statement of the basis of followers of Mr. Fibonacci.

While many Fib proponents believe this, they make an error in their assumption. Retracement theory says that at the common retracement levels, prices find significant resistance to further movement, not that prices must stop there. There is an important distinction between the two! This is a costly mistake that is commonly made by inexperienced traders and technicians. Retracement levels are a good place to put a buy stop or sell stop.

Grab your latte and fasten your seat belt, 'cause here we go.

Figure 14.12, a chart by Jeff Parent, shows the results of a test of where retracement levels came in up moves in S&P 500 stocks. What it

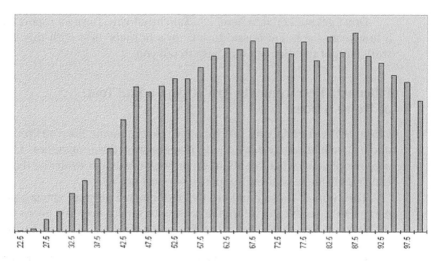

FIGURE 14.12   Fibonacci Retracement Percent Levels
Source: Jeff Parent

shows is that markets can stop in retracement of a rally at almost any point! (Thanks, Jeff, from all of us.)

If Fibonacci was really accurate we should see at least a cluster of these retracements coming at 38 percent, 50 percent, and 62 percent.

Here's what Jeff had to say about his study:

> *This is a histogram showing % retracements from up moving legs. I've used a zigzag function with 20% filter to find tops and bottoms. These represent retracements from local tops. They were culled from the S&P 500 between 1997 and now. 8,000 data points were collected. The histogram steps by 2.5%.*
>
> *I did not use the S&P 500 index; I used the stocks in the S&P 500 index. That's how I got 8,000 data points. For stocks trading below $9, I did see some clustering around the 50% and a couple of other Fib areas. They were visually significant because I could see spikes in the histogram; however, no system could be created to take advantage of this observation. . . . It just doesn't happen often enough.*

What the Chart Shows Me

Well, it's really what the chart does *not* show that bothers me the most here. We should see large clusters of lows coming where those fabulous Fibonacci retracement levels are.

What we see is that markets can retrace to and bounce off just about any percent retracement value. There are no clusters around the Fib numbers. The largest numbers of bounces came at 87.5, a stretch of any basic Fib math. The magic 0.38 shows no ability to stop a decline; 0.62 has no significance to it. I see nothing socially redeeming here, at all, for traders.

And If That's Not Enough

For all I knew, Jeff's study was flawed. I didn't think so, but good research calls for confirmation. My next step was to do a hand test of the S&P 500. I marked off all swings of 5 percent or more with what Genesis Financial Data Services (www.gfds.com) calls their Zig Zag indicator that captures all such swings.

I then looked at two different time periods, 1992–1994 and 2002–2003. I measured each and every rally of more than 5 percent and noted the low following the rally to see what price it stopped at. I then divided the amount of decline into the rally to get the actual percentage of retracement. As the first example (Table 14.1) shows, there was a rally on October 5, 1992, from 696 to 749. The ensuing decline ended at 732, so the math is: (749 − 732) divided by (749 − 696) . . . or 17/53, which equals 32 percent. In this case the answer is close to, but not at, the 38 percent Fibonacci level.

Tables 14.1 and 14.2 show all such rallies and their stopping points for the ensuing corrective wave.

As you can see, I tested 10 rallies in each time period. The results do not support the Fibonacci theory in that out of 20 examples there were only two declines that came close to the Fib numbers, one of 62 percent and one of 35 percent.

TABLE 14.1 Retracement Test for 5 Percent Rallies, 1992–1994

Date	Low	High	Retracement Low	Percent of Pullback
10/5/1992	696	749	732	32
1/8/1993	732	756	754	98
2/18/1993	734	763	737	89
4/26/1993	737	761	737	100
7/6/1993	746	768	753	68
9/21/1993	753	775	758	77
11/5/1993	758	786	736	178
4/4/1994	736	764	739	89
6/24/1994	739	778	747	79
10/5/1994	747	774	741	122
Average				84

TABLE 14.2 Retracement Test for 5 Percent Rallies, 2002–2003

Date	Low	High	Retracement Low	Percent of Pullback
7/24/2002	776	905	825	57
8/5/2002	825	959	863	71
9/5/2002	863	920	809	194
9/24/2002	809	835	792	165
9/30/2002	792	848	761	155
10/10/2002	761	920	864	35
11/13/2002	864	948	862	102
12/30/2002	862	925	800	198
2/13/2003	800	834	783	150
3/12/2003	783	891	837	50
Average				118

The average decline in the 1992–1994 sample was 84 percent, while in the 2002–2003 study the average stopping point was 118 percent of the rallies.

Such a poor showing caused me to test waves of just 2 percent change. Table 14.3 shows that study on 2003 data.

The average decline was 75 percent and there were no direct hits at 0.62 or 0.38. In fact, out of 30 swings, chosen at random, the supposed magic 0.62 and 0.38 numbers appear, plus or minus 1 percent, only two times. A book has been written saying the magic point of retracements is 50 percent. That's where to be a buyer.

Some book, some idea, based on this study. Of the 30 swings, 5

TABLE 14.3 Retracement Test for 2 Percent Rallies, 2003

Date	Low	High	Retracement Low	Percent of Pullback
3/12/2003	783	891	837	50
3/31/2003	837	900	857	68
4/10/2003	857	915	894	36
4/25/2003	894	905	896	81
5/1/2003	896	935	913	56
5/8/2003	913	945	907	118
5/20/2003	907	1,004	968	37
6/9/2003	968	1,011	957	125
7/1/2003	957	1,006	979	55
7/10/2003	979	1,011	970	128
Average				75

stopped between 50 and 60. In other words, not quite 17 percent of the swings bottomed in this supposed "sweet spot" on the charts. The average of all three tests is a pullback of 91 percent!

Finally, I'm presenting a clip of the S&P 500 with the price swings marked off (lines following the pattern of price) and the rallies blocked by the horizontal dashed lines. (See Figure 14.13.) The solid horizontal lines are the all-important Fib numbers, coming down, of 0.38, 0.50, and 0.62. As you can see, while lots of books and advisers claim these levels are surefire buying zones, it appears the market has yet to read these books.

Waking Up Late at Night

Just before I wrote this I was startled from a deep sleep (yeah, right, sure, S&P traders never sleep deeply) with one last thought, that I should try the same test but this time use hourly bars. The Fib crowd is big on these bars (me, I prefer ones overlooking the ocean).

So again I marked off the dominant swing points and am listing them in Table 14.4 from last December through the end of January. I'll let the facts speak for themselves.

Perhaps you can see some rhyme or reason to all these numbers, but for the life of me I cannot. Draw enough lines on a chart and something will happen on one of them. Keep in mind that in this study I measured

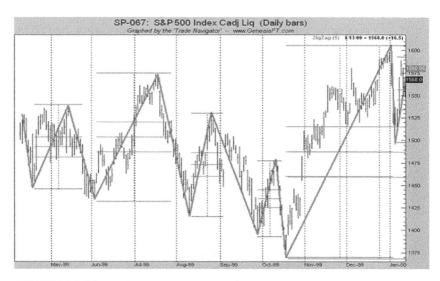

FIGURE 14.13 S&P 500 Index Chart
Source: Genesis Financial Technologies, Inc. (www.GenesisFT.com).

TABLE 14.4 Retracement Test Using 60-Minute Bar Charts

Date	Low	High	Retracement Low	Percent of Pullback
12/4/2004	1,103.5	1,123.5	1,115	42
1/7/2005	1,115	1,130.5	1,119.1	73
1/9/2005	1,119.1	1,128.5	1,114.2	152
1/13/2005	1,114.2	1,142.2	1,133.5	31
1/21/2005	1,133.5	1,149.3	1,135.3	88
1/23/2005	1,135.3	1,155	1,121	172
1/29/2005	1,121	1,133.5	1,126	60
1/30/2005	1,126	1,142	1,123	118
Average				92

only termination of up and down moves (bounces may have occurred along the way) that represent the best buy points, not just little bobbles, which I think makes this study even more important.

A "True Fibber" recently posted this testimonial for the technique. I suggest you read it closely:

> *Protrader that generates automated fib levels using 40 time frames to trade the -minis and the fib levels are uncannily accurate. The same holds true for bonds and currencies. The next challenge once a fib level is hit on the way up and bounced,* is to decide whether it will reverse or turn around and blast up *through it to the next level. But very rarely does price not take a pause and bounce off an automated fib level.*

The emphasis is mine. Isn't that always the question, whether it will go up or down? I think so, which means even something that is "uncannily accurate" is meaningless if it still does not tell us what will happen. Stop and think, folks!

If there is a proper use of Fib retracements, it is to predict where significant resistance to further price movement will occur, not to call the termination of a decline.

Need I say more? Yeah, I will. Don't take my word on this subject; boot up your computer and test for yourself. "Trust but verify" is always the best policy in this business. These numbers may be a tool, but they have no ability to call where the termination of a decline following an up move will take place. Perhaps they can help indicate where a bounce will come, maybe where stops should or should not be placed, but I can find no evidence that markets turn at these magic levels.

Thanks to Jeff Parent, Dave Steckler, and Tom DeMark for input and help on this report.

DON'T MISUNDERSTAND ME ON CHARTS

I most definitely think there is a valid place for keeping and looking at charts. After all, I have done it for the majority of my life. I just admonish you to be careful and take them for what they are: pictures of market activity. I do not think that price itself is the answer to our questions on the art of speculation. The best book I have had the joy to read on speculation, Max Gunther's *Zurich Axioms* (Penguin, 1985), speaks right to the point, warning us to beware the chartist's illusion that a chart, price action, can be a harbinger of the future. You will hear many claims of their powers; I can only urge you to approach such temptations with intellectual curiosity and a healthy dose of skepticism.

When I look for these patterns, my mission is to place them in the context of trend and the COT data, not to use them as stand-alone answers to buying and selling. The longer I have traded and the older I get, the more I see that my earlier mistakes, and ones I continue to make, are all fruit of the same tree; I am not looking at the entire picture, I am trying to make my facts fit as opposed to seeing the broader picture. I might want to tell you, "Tumrw thr will b som mny to be mde at 0 pm that wil be like takng candy fro a bby, com 2 my house."

Hmm, looking at that is like looking at a chart. There are bits and pieces of things you understand or can decipher (chart reading). You think there is some easy money to be made tomorrow in the afternoon. Yes! You can see it. The sentence (chart) even tells you where to go—my house. It's perfectly clear. Except for one thing; what time will all this good stuff take place? Can't tell, can you? Welcome to the world of chart reading.

CHAPTER 15

Putting Theory to Work

Practicing What I Preach

Practice is the best of all instructors.
Publius Syrus (ca. 100 B.C.)

There's not much left to talk about, and I sure don't want to be accused of being "all hat and talk with no cows." So let's turn our attention to some of the major setups that have taken place over the past few years. Surely the future will see similar setups, times when the relationship of open interest (OI) and commercial buying and selling stacks up in the same way, a way you can use to find markets that should have large moves in the direction we know they should.

Ideally, then, and these do not appear every few weeks; they take time, but with 30 active markets to follow you will almost always have a potential trade, a market with OI at low levels while the commercials have been buying.

"Low levels" sounds subjective and it is, so you might want to use the OI tool I described earlier or just look for very low levels. With that in mind, please look at Figure 15.1. Go ahead, look, and if this is your book mark off these points. Oh, you may notice that the chart does not show the price action of bonds. Never mind, we will get to that in a moment, but first I want to make certain you can identify the OI/COT pattern I look for.

Figure 15.1 has been marked off for the commercials with a zero line showing when they are net long, above the zero line, or net short, below the zero line. As you might recall, we are not as concerned with their net position as we are with the relative level of their action. That's why we use the index approach. In Figure 15.2 I have also marked off the high and low levels of total OI during this five-year time span. Hopefully you marked

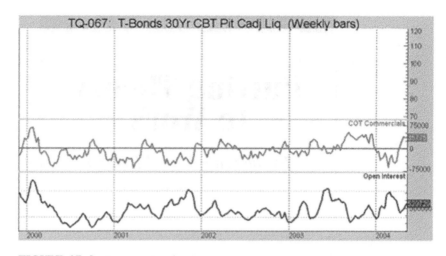

FIGURE 15.1 Treasury Bonds Charts
Source: Genesis Financial Technologies, Inc. (www.GenesisFT.com).

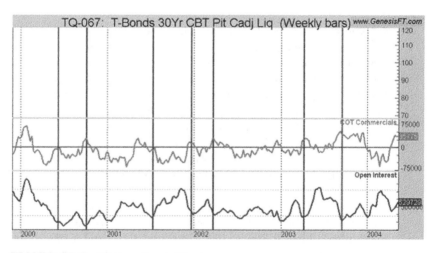

FIGURE 15.2 Treasury Bonds Chart
Source: Genesis Financial Technologies, Inc. (www.GenesisFT.com).

your book along the same lines. Not that I'm the master of this, but I hope we both marked about the same places. If we did, that means you are a good student, I a good teacher, and this material is not mumbo-jumbo stuff that is wildly subjective.

Well, how did you do? Did most of your lines come at about the same points as mine? I'm betting they did. Good going! I like to trade the U.S. bond market because the margin is low, it correlates well with other markets, and it has pretty decent volume so I can get in and out, usually, without too many problems. The setups occur with a degree of regularity and almost anyone, once they know what to look for, can spot them, as you just did. Are we ready to buy at those junctures?

ONE MORE STEP TO MASTER

There is one more key ingredient . . . the trend of the market. I deliberately did not show the price of the bond market as I want you to realize that we do not have to look at price action, nor do we need to decipher chart patterns of price. The patterns that prevail, as I see it, are the patterns of the underpinnings of the market OI and COT. The next step is easy; we just have to figure out if price is in an uptrend at the junctures we have marked off.

Was price in an uptrend or a downtrend? What is trend? How can we see it with more clarity? These are all good questions, and like all good questions easier to ask than answer, yet there are answers. Since we are looking at weekly charts we could use a long-term moving average of weekly closing prices to help us see the true trend direction. That's exactly what the next clip shows: a 39-week moving average of bond prices . . . and so far we are not looking at bond prices. They will be the last thing at which we look, as price can be so deceptive. The moving average line will be up, down, or flat. If it is down we cannot buy, if up we can, if flat and prices are down we can buy, and finally if the weekly price is above the moving average the trend is up so we can buy.

Figure 15.3 is the moving average chart sans bond prices to help you further select points to look for market entries.

Any doubts now as to what the trend was? It sure makes it easier to look at the average of price, rather than just price. Last, let's look at the full picture so you can see where the setups took place and what bond prices did following the OI/COT pattern I have taught you to look for (see Figure 15.4). You may also note the potential profit just one of the setups offered a follower of this thesis. This is not unusual; what is unusual is for a trader or speculator to ride the entire move that long.

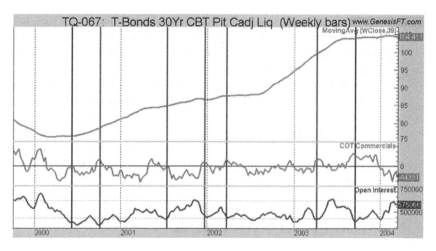

FIGURE 15.3 Treasury Bonds Chart
Source: Genesis Financial Technologies, Inc. (www.GenesisFT.com).

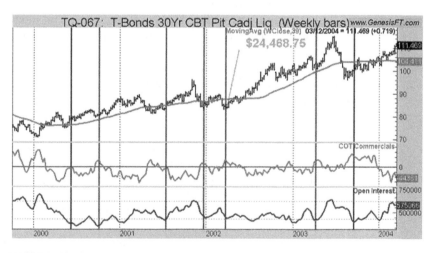

FIGURE 15.4 Treasury Bonds Chart
Source: Genesis Financial Technologies, Inc. (www.GenesisFT.com).

A DIFFERENT VIEW OF THE SAME PROBLEM

We are going to play this game a little longer . . . and I suggest you really do go through this exercise, as it is how you learn and imprint these techniques on your mind. We will start with a chart with OI and the COT net position, the same as we did in bonds, but this time I'm not even going to tell you the market. Just mark the times OI is low and the COT position high on a relative basis. Let's do that now (see Figure 15.5).

I'm doing the same exercise as you, so I'll show you what I marked off as times when the bullish COT/OI pattern appeared on the chart, as I see it. I wish I could be right there with you to see how close we came to coming up with the same answer! Figure 15.6 shows how I called it.

Do we agree? Are the vertical lines I marked off the same as yours? Do you agree that my markings show when the COT indicated buying and OI was at a low level? I sure hope so. Heck, I'm pretty sure they did—this is not rocket science.

All that's left is to look at the price trend to see which of these setups we would have used for buying whatever this commodity is. Here it is in Figure 15.7.

Hey, look at that! There were times the setups were there but price was in a downtrend so we could not have used them for entries. Dang, I wanted to buy long and for five years was not able to. If we could not have bought, could we have sold short? Well, yes, if OI is high and the COT net

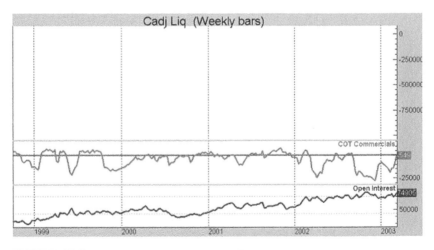

FIGURE 15.5 Chart with Open Interest and COT Net Position
Source: Genesis Financial Technologies, Inc. (www.GenesisFT.com).

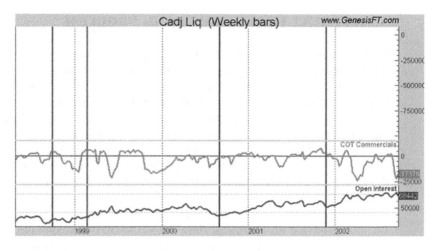

FIGURE 15.6   Marked Chart
Source: Genesis Financial Technologies, Inc. (www.GenesisFT.com).

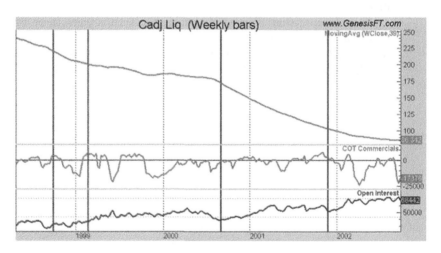

FIGURE 15.7   Chart with Trend View
Source: Genesis Financial Technologies, Inc. (www.GenesisFT.com).

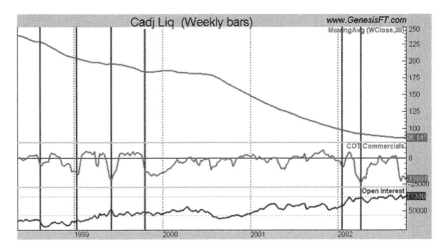

FIGURE 15.8 Marked Chart with Trend View
Source: Genesis Financial Technologies, Inc. (www.GenesisFT.com).

reading shows the commercials have been selling. With that in mind I have marked off Figure 15.8 to show the potential sell setups. We know the trend called for selling, but the issue is whether there are any sell setups.

As I went over the chart I marked off six times when the COT was relatively low while OI was relatively high. In five years there were only six times we had 'em right where we wanted 'em, in a picture-perfect setup of the three strongest factors in the marketplace: trend, the superpowers (COT), and the usually wrong public (OI). I guess we had better take a look now at what happened, how it actually panned out in real time, how the truth unfolded (see Figure 15.9).

First of all, let me identify the market; what we have been looking at is coffee. Typically this is a wild and wooly market, not highly liquid so there is lots of slippage, and characterized by very fast, explosive moves. It is not a market for first-time traders. But my stuff works there as well as in any other market. The rules bypassed all the buys, thanks to Mr. Trend, while five of the six sell setups were right on the button. The one at the end of 1999 was premature but did lead to one of the largest declines in the history of coffee.

Had we had the wisdom to sell one contract of coffee in late 1999, the potential for profits was more than $34,000 on a $1,500 investment. Great odds, clearly foretold by our tools. Could you have held on that long? I doubt it; I did not.

I could go on and on with these examples, but it will be better if you grab a chart book or open up your computer to check out and learn the

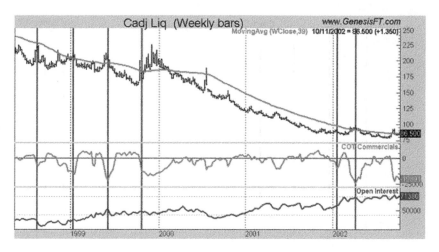

FIGURE 15.9 Price Chart
Source: Genesis Financial Technologies, Inc. (www.GenesisFT.com).

power of these patterns. There are several software providers, such as TradeStation or eSignal, that have much of this data, but the most complete place is Genesis Financial Data Services (www.gfds.com). I think it's better to spend money and time learning these tools, without trading, than to try to jump into the thick of things. You can also go to www.ireally trade.com and I will show more examples in my Larry Live videos.

There will always be markets, and there will always be opportunities. Time is on your side. Master the art and craft of trading before you begin, then "let 'er rip."

I hope you have enjoyed this book, that it will be helpful to you and your family, and that our paths cross in the future.

Index

Printed and bound by CPI Group (UK) Ltd, Croydon, CR0 4YY

16/04/2025

14658508-0001